Tom Clancy's GHOST RECON

Volume 30

Written by:

The Stratos Group:

Jessi Conrad • Noah Conrad

Brett Norton • Zack Schiel

Art Design and Layout:

Eric Castellanos • Karen Mui

•Casandra Mack • Stephanie Zavadil

•Debbie Wells

CEO
Matthew Taylor

President
Len Ciciretto

VP of Editorial and Associate Publisher
Howard Grossman

Production Director
Peter Discoe

VP of Sales
Skip McFerran

Controller
Janice Raab

Assistant Controller
Patti Leigh

Sales Assistant
Kay Smith

Webmaster / IT Specialist
Renee Malcolm

Administrative Assistant
Shamika Guidry

Accounting Assistant
Jacque Davidson

Corporate Advisor
Patrick J. Ferrell

Newsstand Consultants
PSCS

Printed in USA
ISBN no. 0-9706468-9-5

Tell us what you thought of this book
email: ghostrecon@versusbooks.com
web:versusbooks.com
snail mail: Ghost Recon
c/o Versus Books PMB #404
2532 Santa Clara Ave.
Alameda, Ca. 94501-4634

Tom Clancy's GHOST RECON

VERSUS BOOKS PERFECT GUIDE

TABLE OF CONTENTS

Introduction

If you're unfamiliar with Rainbow Six and Rogue Spear, the other Tom Clancy games developed by Red Storm, the gameplay of Ghost Recon might come as a shock to you. Unlike most standard first-person games, Ghost Recon attempts to simulate modern military missions with realistic details. Whereas the playable characters in most first-person games can absorb an unrealistic amount of punishment and are expected to simultaneously fight off overwhelming numbers of enemies, the soldiers of Ghost Recon are as susceptible to bullets and grenades as a normal human is, and they are incapable of fighting off an army of enemy soldiers (usually) at once.

The tactical planning in Ghost Recon also sets it apart from most first-person games. Instead of a single main character, the player must coordinate the efforts of multiple soldiers to achieve many of his goals. While it is quite possible to complete many missions relying on only a single soldier type of your choice, there are times when you must split your forces to simultaneously defend or attack separate objectives. These situations require you to become familiar with many different soldier roles,

unless you are dead set on completing the mission with a specific soldier. You may be a tiny god with a sniper rifle, but you will inevitably find yourself in a situation where you can't snipe the enemy and must change tactics.

This guide was designed with one objective in mind: To give you an edge in Ghost Recon over those who do not have this guide. Whereas most players will be capable of delving into the missions (both single and multiplayer) and figuring out how to play efficiently, this book is here to give you an upper hand over them, or at least a noticeable head start. We hope that you learn a lot from this guide, and can use this knowledge to your advantage.

Chapter 2 begins with a rundown of the various soldiers in Ghost Recon and what they do. A breakdown of the soldiers by class, an in-depth look at the soldiers' individual statistics, and a glimpse of the game's hidden specialist characters are all covered in this section.

Chapter 3 gives you a tour of the weapons and other equipment used by your soldiers. The different guns, ranging from the M9 Pistol to the MG3 Machine Gun, are broken down and analyzed. Additionally, the non-gun tools in Ghost Recon, such as M67 Frag Grenades and the AN/GSQ-187 Sensor, are covered in this section.

Chapter 4 is where strategic and tactical analysis is spelled out. Every tactic, tip, hint, and strategy we've picked up and formulated while playing Ghost Recon is analyzed and broken down. General strategies, such as troop placement and movement, as well as more specific terrain tactics, are detailed here.

Chapter 5 is a walk-through of every single-player Campaign mission in Ghost Recon. If you're having trouble beating one of the missions, turning to this section for information on troop locations, recommended strategies, and other useful info may help break a stalemate in your progression. Be warned, however, that this section contains some spoiler information that may dilute your Ghost Recon single-player experience. We recommend that

you use it as an aid when you're having severe trouble progressing rather than an in-hand guide through the game.

Chapter 6 runs through the Recon and Firefight variant missions. By the time you have unlocked a few Quick Missions to experiment with Recon and Firefight, you should have a firm understanding of how to play Ghost Recon. This section is mainly aimed at providing tips and suggestions for players already familiar with specific maps.

Chapter 7 takes one more look at the maps in Ghost Recon, this time for their multiplayer potential. All of the Campaign maps, and several additional multiplayer-only maps, are covered in this section. You don't necessarily need to have played all the missions in the regular campaign to understand this section; it's targeted to reach both players who are and players who are not familiar with the game's maps.

Thanks for reading, and good luck.

INTRODUCTION

CHAPTER 2
The Soldiers

The soldiers in Ghost Recon encompass quite a broad diversity of talents and skills. This section will provide you with information on who the soldiers are and how they measure up statistically to the rest of the game's soldiers.

Each soldier in Ghost Recon is classified by four statistics: Weapon, Endurance, Stealth, and Leadership. Understanding what each of these values means can help you choose the best combination of soldiers to form your squads. Whenever a soldier survives a campaign mission, he earns a single Combat Point that he can spend in any of these four stats to permanently raise the stat by one. If you use a soldier from start to finish throughout the campaign, even the initial soldiers you begin with can have impressive stats by the end of the game. Try to build up a core group of soldiers that you can use on every mission that all have excellent stats. Many of the specialists (more on those later) will replace your need for the original soldiers, but you'll still want to pick a couple specialists to turn into hardened combat veterans. What the stats do, and some tips on how to spend your earned Combat Points, follows.

Weapon

The Weapon stat does not directly determine how accurate your soldiers are with their guns; it works in a rather indirect fashion. Whenever your soldiers move or fire their guns, their weapon pips are pushed away from the center of your crosshairs, indicating that the recoil or jerkiness of movement is throwing off their aim. The higher a soldier's weapon skill, the quicker these pips return to the center of your crosshairs. Each additional point in Weapon skill beyond the first decreases the time it takes for the weapon pips to re-center by 10%. While a modest weapon will benefit all your soldiers, it is not necessary for a soldier to have an extremely high Weapon skill to be effective. Snipers, whose sniper rifles are prone to having their weapon pips thrown very far off-center by movement, benefit heavily from a high Weapon skill. With most other classes and guns, however, you can get by with a 4–6 Weapon skill quite acceptably. Overall, weapon skill is probably the second most important stat.

Endurance

Endurance is the number of times a soldier can be wounded before he simply collapses from the excessive amount of damage he has taken. Each additional point of Endurance increases by one the number of wounds a soldier can take before dying. While it's rather helpful to have at least a few extra points in Endurance to help reduce the odds that a stray shot

will take out your favorite soldier, anything more than 3–4 points in Endurance really isn't terribly useful. Most of the time, when your soldier takes fire, he gets hammered very quickly by a lot of firepower and has little chance of surviving. Endurance is useful in small amounts, but don't worry about increasing it to the higher levels. Use your points for Stealth instead; it's a much more useful stat for defense.

Stealth

If there is one stat that matters more than any other, it is the Stealth stat. There are two basic functions of the Stealth stat. The first, and probably less important, is that the higher the soldier's Stealth stat, the closer he can sneak up on an enemy without the enemy detecting him. The default minimum distance you can get to an enemy before he automatically becomes aware of your presence is 10 meters. Each point of Stealth a soldier has reduces this distance by one meter. This is mainly only important when fighting indoors or in other such cramped conditions. Second, the Stealth stat decreases the range at which enemy soldiers will spot you while you are moving. Once your soldiers start getting high Stealth stats (6+) you can practically run up on enemy soldiers and shoot them from less than 40 m away, depending on light conditions. Stealth, as discussed in the Strategy and Tactics chapter, is your most important defensive asset, so you should try to get all your soldiers up to at least a five in this skill. It also helps immensely to group your squads by comparable Stealth stats; a lone soldier in a squad who's bad at stealth might spoil the entire squad's sneak attack.

Leadership

Every good platoon needs a strong leader. In game terms, the Leadership stat acts as a bonus that the soldier shares with everyone else in his squad. However, only the soldier with the highest Leadership stat gets to apply his bonus. For every point of Leadership the soldier with the highest Leadership has, he increases his own and all his platoon's stats by one-third of a point. This means three points of Leadership equates to a full point in every other stat. Having multiple strong leaders won't do you a ton of good; it's better to concentrate on getting one good soldier with a high Leadership and then develop one or two lesser leaders. A lot of the later specialists have a high Leadership stat, so you can wait until you have one of those and spend your Combat Points in the meantime pumping up your soldiers' Stealth and Weapon stats.

Basic Classes

There are four basic soldier classes in Ghost Recon. The most significant difference between each class is its equipment. A brief rundown of each of the classes and a list of the game's specialists follows, but for more in-depth information on the equipment, see Chapter 3.

RIFLEMAN

The Rifleman is the most versatile of all the classes. While he lacks any specific specialization, his equipment is suited for all types of engagements. Although he can't carry M67 Frag Grenades like all the other classes, he is the only class that can carry the M203 Grenade Launcher. It's exceptionally hard to run through all your M16A2 ammunition in one mission, so either the M203 or the M9-SD is your best bet as a secondary weapon. The Rifleman can be best viewed as the medium-range class in Ghost Recon.

CLASS RIFLEMAN

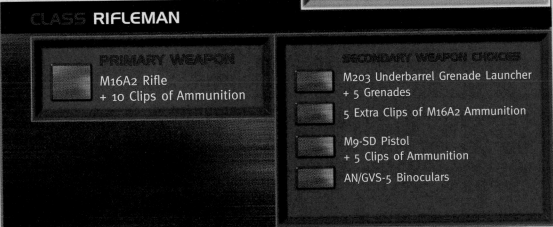

PRIMARY WEAPON

M16A2 Rifle
+ 10 Clips of Ammunition

SECONDARY WEAPON CHOICES

M203 Underbarrel Grenade Launcher
+ 5 Grenades

5 Extra Clips of M16A2 Ammunition

M9-SD Pistol
+ 5 Clips of Ammunition

AN/GVS-5 Binoculars

SUPPORT

Support soldiers pack a light machine gun, sacrificing a bit of stealth, accuracy, and range for sheer firepower. Their M249 LMG emits a lot of noise and makes them a prime target for enemy soldiers. However, their gun does have a huge ammo capacity and can fire on full auto for extended bursts without as severe a loss of accuracy as many other weapons. Support soldiers, as close-range specialists, are a bit harder to keep alive than your other troops; don't overuse them in your squads. Frag Grenades make great secondary weapon choices, because they give Support soldiers a bit of indirect-fire capability.

CLASS **SUPPORT**

PRIMARY WEAPON

M249 Light Machine Gun
+ 3 Clips of Ammunition

SECONDARY WEAPON CHOICES

2 Extra Clips of M249 Ammunition

6 M67 Frag Grenades

M9-SD Pistol
+ 5 Clips of Ammunition

AN/GVS-5 Binoculars

SNIPER

In contrast to the close-range capability of the Support soldier, Snipers excel at long-range combat. Their basic weapon, the M24, has five times the zooming power of a normal rifle, allowing them to engage enemy soldiers from a much longer range. However, their lack of a rapid-fire medium- or close-range weapon puts them at a severe disadvantage when spotted. Snipers rely a lot on stealth and speed; try to avoid being spotted whenever possible. Probably the best secondary weapon for the Sniper is the M9-SD, a silenced weapon that gives them a little more versatility at close range and can enable them to clear a building out with surprising efficiency.

CLASS **SNIPER**

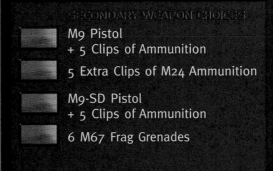

PRIMARY WEAPON

M24 Sniper Rifle
+ 10 Clips of Ammunition

SECONDARY WEAPON CHOICES

M9 Pistol
+ 5 Clips of Ammunition

5 Extra Clips of M24 Ammunition

M9-SD Pistol
+ 5 Clips of Ammunition

6 M67 Frag Grenades

DEMOLITIONS

Unlike the other three classes, which could be roughly separated into close, medium, and long-range combatants, Demolitions soldiers exist mainly to fulfill specific mission functions. Their main weapon is a slightly weaker version of the M16, but you'll probably never notice the difference. Demolitions soldiers have two specific secondary weapons available to them, the M136 Anti-Tank Rocket Launcher and the M2 Demolition Charges. The M2 Demolition Charges are only useful for completing mission goals, so take them only when a mission calls for them. On the other hand, the M136 can be used to fulfill mission objectives, and also serves as a nice anti-infantry weapon. While it may not be as versatile as the Riflemen's M203 Grenade Launcher, the M136 is very powerful—a single rocket can clear out a building or enemy bunker quite effectively. If you don't need the M2 Demolition Charges for the mission, definitely take the M136 as your secondary weapon. A special note here is in order: of the two Demolitions specialists, one carries M136 Anti-Tank Rockets and another carries M2 Demolition Charges. As a result, if you wish to have a powerful soldier who is capable of using both, then you will need to build up a single regular Demolitions soldier from the beginning of the campaign to the end. This can be very important, because one of the later missions will require you to have two soldiers capable of laying demolitions charges in order to complete the optional objective.

CLASS DEMOLITION

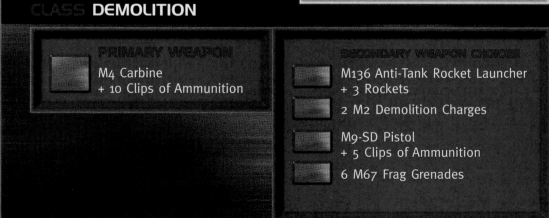

PRIMARY WEAPON

M4 Carbine
+ 10 Clips of Ammunition

SECONDARY WEAPON CHOICES

M136 Anti-Tank Rocket Launcher
+ 3 Rockets

2 M2 Demolition Charges

M9-SD Pistol
+ 5 Clips of Ammunition

6 M67 Frag Grenades

SPECIALISTS

The specialists in Ghost Recon are infinitely more interesting than the regular soldiers and tend to be capable of far more. While they are modeled after the basic soldier classes, they often have superior stats and advanced special weapons. If one of your specialists dies during a mission, he will not be replaced, so be very careful about sacrificing one of your favorite specialists. The specialists are unlocked in a sequential order; you unlock a specific specialist for each mission. If you miss unlocking a specialist, you will have to replay that mission in order to unlock him. If you really want to get all the specialists (and you probably do), make sure that you unlock a new specialist during each mission. Unlocking a specialist involves completing the specific bonus mission objective in addition to the regular mission objectives.

CLASS RIFLEMAN
ORDER UNLOCKED 1st

WILL JACOBS

Will Jacobs

The first specialist you unlock is Will Jacobs. The truly important feature of this Rifleman specialist is the powerful OICW Rifle he uses. While the base OICW Rifle acts a lot like the M16A2, the OICW's semi-automatic grenade launcher (found in the secondary weapon slot) is vastly superior to the M16A2's M203 Grenade Launcher. Since you unlock Will early in the campaign, you have plenty of time to build up his stats. If you're willing to drag him along on every mission, he can easily become one of your best soldiers toward the end of the campaign.

PRIMARY WEAPON

OICW Rifle
+ 10 Clips of Ammunition

SECONDARY WEAPON CHOICES

OICW Grenade Launcher
+ 2 Clips of Ammunition

AN/GVS-5 Binoculars

M9-SD Pistol
+ 5 Clips of Ammunition

5 Extra Clips of OICW Rifle Ammunition

WEAPON: 3

●●● ○○○○○○ +

STEALTH: 2

●● ○○○○○○○ +

ENDURANCE: 2

●● ○○○○○○○ +

LEADERSHIP: 3

●●● ○○○○○○ +

Combat Points = 00

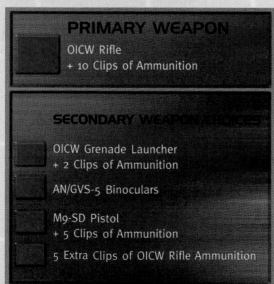

CLASS RIFLEMAN
ORDER UNLOCKED 2nd

HENRY RAMIREZ

Henry Ramirez

Henry Ramirez isn't overwhelmingly powerful when you first unlock him, but he can become one of the most dangerous specialists if you use him correctly. The main advantage of Henry is his nasty MP5-SD, a fairly powerful, accurate, and silent weapon. If you use Henry in every mission and continue to pump up his Stealth and Weapon stats, he can become the game's most dangerous assassin. In addition to his special primary gun, Henry can use both Claymore Mines and Sensors. While he might lack the long reach of other Riflemen, his silenced weapon and special booby-trap equipment make Henry Ramirez one of the best specialists in the game.

PRIMARY WEAPON

MP5-SD Submachine Gun
+ 10 Clips of Ammunition

SECONDARY WEAPON CHOICES

2 M18 Claymore Mines

5 Extra Clips of MP5-SD Ammunition

M9-SD Pistol
+ 5 Clips of Ammunition

2 AN/GSQ-187 Sensors

WEAPON: 3

STEALTH: 2

ENDURANCE: 3

LEADERSHIP: 3

Combat Points = 00

SPECIALIST

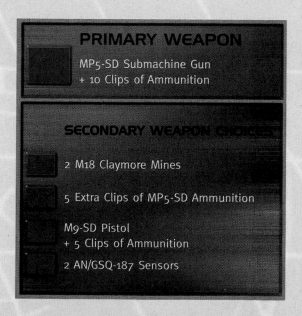

CLASS DEMOLITIONS
ORDER UNLOCKED 3rd

NIGEL TUNNEY

Nigel Tunney

Nigel packs the unique SA80 Carbine and can carry four Anti-Tank Rockets instead of the normal three, but unfortunately he can't use M2 Demolition Charges. Nigel is a nice step up from the regular Demolitions soldiers  at the start of the campaign, but unless you want to have him tag along on missions that don't require his Anti-Tank Rockets, he really isn't a wise long-term investment. Nigel Tunney and Klaus Henkel are counterparts; if you're going to use Nigel you'll probably also want to start using Klaus when you unlock him. By using them together you'll be able to avoid using an underpowered normal Demolitions soldier for later missions that require M2 Demolition Charges.

WEAPON: 4
●●●●○○○○○ +

STEALTH: 3
●●●○○○○○○ +

ENDURANCE: 3
●●●○○○○○○ +

LEADERSHIP: 2
●●○○○○○○○ +

Combat Points = 00

PRIMARY WEAPON

SA80 Carbine
+ 10 Clips of Ammunition

SECONDARY WEAPON CHOICES

M136 Anti-Tank Rocket Launcher
+ 4 Rockets

6 M67 Frag Grenades

M9-SD Pistol
+ 5 Clips of Ammunition

2 M18 Claymore Mines

CLASS SNIPER
ORDER UNLOCKED 4th

JACK STONE

Jack Stone

Jack is pretty much a loner Sniper. His Leadership stat is base, but his Weapon and Stealth skills are high for when you get him. It is rather unfortunate that you get Jack  Stone so early, because obtaining him early immediately makes your regular Snipers obsolete. Jack Stone becomes your default Sniper in Ghost Recon, simply because he's so good and the other two Sniper specialists aren't unlocked until much later in the game. You can use Jack throughout most of the game, and by campaign's end it's easy to max both his Weapon and Stealth stats. He gets a little overshadowed by the later specialists Astra Galinsky and Scott Ibrahim, but he's still a worthwhile specialist to build up.

WEAPON: 4

STEALTH: 5

ENDURANCE: 3

LEADERSHIP: 1

Combat Points = 00

PRIMARY WEAPON

L96A1 Sniper Rifle
+ 10 Clips of Ammunition

SECONDARY WEAPON CHOICES

M9 Pistol
+ 5 Clips of Ammunition

5 Extra Clips of L96A1 Ammunition

M9-SD Pistol
+ 5 Clips of Ammunition

6 M67 Frag Grenades

SPECIALIST

GURAM OSADZE

SPECIALIST

Guram Osadze

Unlike the more balanced specialists you unlock earlier, Guram has some pretty tilted stats. His Weapon and Endurance stats are high up there,  but his Stealth stat is the minimum. Fortunately, if you want to develop Guram Osadze into a well-rounded warrior, you have plenty of time in the campaign to do so. Guram is equipped with a Russian support LMG, the RPK74. Guram Osadze might not be as versatile as your normal support troops when you unlock him, but use him early and often and he gets very powerful by the campaign's end.

WEAPON: 5

STEALTH: I

ENDURANCE: 5

LEADERSHIP: 3

Combat Points = OO

PRIMARY WEAPON

RPK74 Light Machine Gun
+ 4 Clips of Ammunition

SECONDARY WEAPON CHOICE

2 Extra Clips of RPK74 Ammunition

AN/GVS-5 Binoculars

M9-SD Pistol
+ 5 Clips of Ammunition

6 M67 Frag Grenades

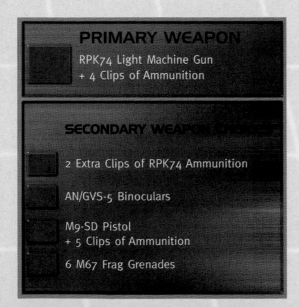

CLASS RIFLEMAN
ORDER UNLOCKED 6th

Susan Grey

Susan Grey is a Rifleman in the same vein as specialist Henry Ramirez. She comes equipped with the silenced MP5-SD and the  odd assortment of Claymores and Sensors. If you've been using Henry Ramirez rather thoroughly since you got him, you may not need Susan Grey at all. Susan has good stats, and if you like silenced weaponry you'll love her, but if you only need one silent assassin you might as well stick with Henry. If you have lost Ramirez in combat, however, then Susan Grey will become extremely attractive.

SUSAN GREY

WEAPON: 3
● ● ● ○ ○ ○ ○ ○ ○   +

STEALTH: 5
● ● ● ● ● ○ ○ ○ ○   +

ENDURANCE: 5
● ● ● ● ● ○ ○ ○ ○   +

LEADERSHIP: 2
● ● ○ ○ ○ ○ ○ ○ ○   +

Combat Points = 00

SPECIALIST

PRIMARY WEAPON

MP5-SD Submachine Gun
+ 10 Clips of Ammunition

SECONDARY WEAPON CHOICES

5 Extra Clips of
MP5-SD Ammunition

2 M18 Claymore Mines

M9-SD Pistol
+ 5 Clips of Ammunition

2 AN/GSQ-187 Sensors

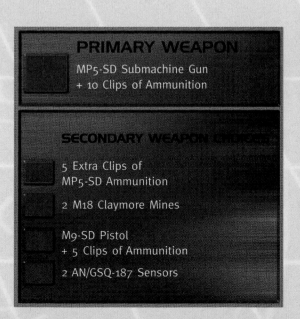

CLASS DEMOLITIONS
ORDER UNLOCKED 7th

KLAUS HENKEL

Klaus Henkel

Unlike every other specialist equipped with an MP5, Klaus does not use a silencer on his gun. This has the unfortunate effect of making him less desirable than either Susan Grey or Henry Ramirez, but he's not without his own charms. Klaus is the only Demolitions specialist who packs M2 Demolition Charges, so if you haven't been pumping up a regular Demolitions soldier for use in the later missions that require M2 Demolition Charges, you will have to use Klaus. Apart from his M2 Demolition Charges though, Klaus carries double the normal allotment of Mines and Sensors. In all honesty, Klaus is only useful if you don't have a pumped-up regular Demolitions soldier, so you'll either love him or you'll find him useless. Klaus really is part of a two-man team with specialist Nigel Tunney, so either use both or use a pumped-up normal Demolitions soldier instead.

WEAPON: 4

STEALTH: 4

ENDURANCE: 4

LEADERSHIP: 4

Combat Points = 00

PRIMARY WEAPON

MP5 Submachine Gun
+ 10 Clips of Ammunition

SECONDARY WEAPON CHOICES

2 M2 Demolition Charges

4 M18 Claymore Mines

M9-SD Pistol
+ 5 Clips of Ammunition

4 AN/GSQ-187 Sensors

BUZZ GORDON

Buzz Gordon

Buzz is a bit of an oddity in the Ghost Recon specialist list. The main reason he's an oddity is because he's not really special. Unlike the  other Riflemen specialists, Buzz Gordon packs the standard M16A2 of normal Riflemen, and he doesn't really have much else going for him. While his Weapon and Leadership stats are great, his Stealth stat is abysmally low for a character unlocked so late in the game. If you don't already have a dedicated leader character, or you have lost your previous one, Buzz Gordon can fill in nicely. Otherwise, however, there's no real reason to use Buzz.

WEAPON: 5

STEALTH: 3

ENDURANCE: 4

LEADERSHIP: 5

Combat Points = 00

PRIMARY WEAPON

M16A2 Rifle
+ 10 Clips of Ammunition

SECONDARY WEAPON

M203 Underbarrel Grenade Launcher
+ 5 Grenades

AN/GVS-5 Binoculars

M9-SD Pistol
+ 5 Clips of Ammunition

5 Extra Clips of M16A2 Ammunition

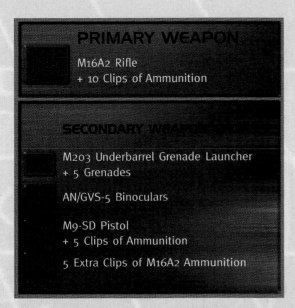

CLASS RIFLEMAN
ORDER UNLOCKED 9th

Lindy Cohen

If Will Jacobs has died in battle, Lindy Cohen is your only hope for another OICW Rifle. Essentially, she's exactly like Will, but with pumped-up base stats. If you've kept Will Jacobs alive and taken him on a fair number of missions, however, odds are that his stats will be close to or better than those of Lindy Cohen. There's not a strong incentive to use Lindy, but if you really want to use another OICW in combat, she's there for you.

PRIMARY WEAPON

OICW Rifle
+ 10 Clips of Ammunition

SECONDARY WEAPON CHOICES

OICW Grenade Launcher
+ 2 Clips of Ammunition

AN/GVS-5 Binoculars

M9-SD Pistol
+ 5 Clips of Ammunition

5 Extra Clips of OICW Rifle Ammunition

LINDY COHEN

WEAPON: 6

STEALTH: 4

ENDURANCE: 3

LEADERSHIP: 5

Combat Points = 00

ASTRA GALINSKY

Astra Galinsky

This Russian
Sniper is one of
the last specialists
you unlock and
comes with a
unique sniper rifle,
the SVD. Unlike
any of the

previous snipers' rifles used in the game, Astra's
SVD is semi-automatic and has an extra zoom
level. Astra Galinsky is also pretty pumped up
stat-wise, and if you begin using her
immediately, you can max out her Weapon and
Stealth stats quickly.

WEAPON: 6

STEALTH: 6

ENDURANCE: 4

LEADERSHIP: 3

Combat Points = 00

PRIMARY WEAPON

SVD Dragunov Sniper Rifle
+ 10 Clips of Ammunition

SECONDARY WEAPON

M9 Pistol + 5 Clips of Ammunition

5 Extra Clips of SVD Ammunition

M9-SD Pistol
+ 5 Clips of Ammunition

6 M67 Frag Grenades

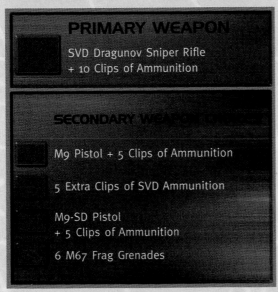

SPECIALIST

SPECIALIST

CLASS SNIPER
ORDER UNLOCKED 11th

Scott Ibrahim

Scott's Weapon and
Stealth stats are
unmatched, and his
M82A1 Sniper Rifle
is semi-automatic
and has a second
zoom feature like
Astra Galinsky's

SVD. Depending on the number of Snipers you
use in your average squad, you may or may not
need Scott Ibrahim. Astra Galinsky, if you've
packed some combat experience on her, should
be roughly comparable stat-wise to Scott when
you unlock him. If you are using only one Sniper,
you can either stick with Astra or switch to Scott.
If you used Jack Stone in every mission, he will
probably have better stats than either Astra or
Scott at this point, but the superior Sniper
rifles of Astra and Scott really make them more
attractive than Jack Stone.

PRIMARY WEAPON

M82A1 Rifle
+ 10 Clips of Ammunition

SECONDARY

M9 Pistol
+5 Clips of Ammunition

M9-SD Pistol
+ 5 Clips of Ammunition

5 Extra Clips of M82A1 Ammunition

6 M67 Frag Grenades

SCOTT IBRAHIM

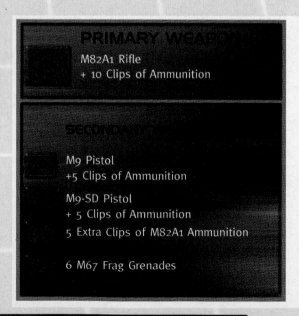

WEAPON: 7

●●●●●●●● ○ +

STEALTH: 7

●●●●●●●● ○ +

ENDURANCE: 4

●●●● ○○○○○ +

LEADERSHIP: 2

●● ○○○○○○ +

Combat Points = 00

Dieter Munz

As far as Endurance goes, Dieter Munz wins the competition hands down. There is no real reason to have a character with an Endurance  stat this high, but it's interesting to see one nonetheless. Unfortunately, Dieter's Stealth stat is ridiculously low for when you get him, even with his leadership bonus. Mixing Dieter in with your regular forces can be a problem, as his lack of Stealth has a tendency to draw a lot of fire onto his squad. Dieter is really a skilled specialist, but you'll have your hands full keeping him alive. If you use him, start putting your combat points into his Stealth stat immediately.

PRIMARY WEAPON

MG3 Light Machine Gun
+ 6 Clips of Ammunition

SECONDARY WEAPON

3 Extra Clips of MG3 Ammunition

6 M67 Frag Grenades

M9-SD Pistol
+ 5 Clips of Ammunition

AN/GVS-5 Binoculars

DIETER MUNZ

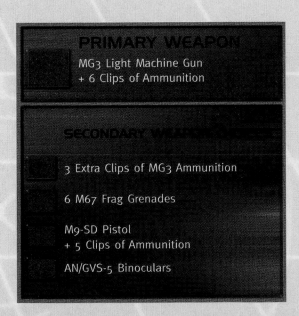

WEAPON: 7

STEALTH: 1

ENDURANCE: 7

LEADERSHIP: 6

Combat Points = 00

SPECIALIST

FIRETEAM STRUCTURE

Standard campaign missions allow you to use up to six soldiers divided into a maximum of three squads. While you can use less than the six maximum, you might as well take all six on each mission to increase the number of soldiers you have who earn Combat Points. There are three basic setups you can choose from while creating your fireteams.

2-2-2

By putting two soldiers in each fireteam, you're given the maximum amount of flexibility in moving your soldiers around. This makes it easy to group soldiers with like stats together, and also allows you to micromanage your squad fairly uniformly. This formation lacks any specific strong point, but it also lacks any real weaknesses.

1-2-3

Using this setup, you can put a single "special" soldier into a squad by himself and still have two larger fireteams for bigger battles. If you have a favorite soldier you like to control yourself, such as a Sniper or a soldier with a silenced gun, you can single him out so he's not assigned to a an otherwise incompatible fireteam. For players who like to get into the action and not have to worry so much about accidentally leading a team member into harm's way, this is the best setup.

3-3

The only real advantage of this formation is that you'll have the maximum amount of soldiers in each fireteam covering their teammates' backs. Also, since you'll be in control of one of the fireteams, you only have to worry about managing one other fireteam on the Command Screen at a time. You should only really try this formation if you have a lot of soldiers with similar abilities, such as running a Sniper fireteam and a Support fireteam who cover each other's backs.

CHAPTER 3
Weaponry and Equipment

CHAPTER 3
Weapons and Equipment

The weapons of Ghost Recon are mostly straightforward guns, with several slight exceptions. While all have similar basic ballistic capabilities, however, there are large variations in how each of the guns performs in combat. The guns, and other weapons and equipment in Ghost Recon, are covered in depth in this section. There are several statistics listed for each weapon, some of which require the following explanations.

ACCURACY TABLE

Each gun's weapon pips do not behave in exactly the same fashion. Some guns can be used effectively on the move; others require the user to remain nearly motionless to be effective. The table for each gun indicates the minimum distances their pips can converge to while in the various types of movement in each stance. The higher the number, the less accurate the gun is in that stance.

Note that while moving, guns are more accurate in the Standing stance than either of the other two stances. This has an especially big impact in multiplayer, where speed is more important than in single-player. You can't actually run while prone, so it uses the same value as though you were trying to walk.

ACCURACY TABLE	STATIONARY	SHUFFLING	WALKING	RUNNING
PRONE	5	45	400	400
CROUCH	8	60	100	750
STAND	10	80	50	500

ACCURACY TABLE	STATIONARY	SHUFFLING	WALKING	RUNNING	FIRE MODES & ROF	
PRONE	7	50	450	450	SINGLE SHOT	ROF 700
CROUCH	10	80	120	800	3 ROUND BURST	ROF 700
STAND	15	37.5	60	600	RECOIL	
KILL POWER					40	
HEAD	99%	LOWER ARM	61%		STABILIZATION TIME	
CHEST	94%	UPPER LEG	72%		25 SECONDS	
ABDOMEN	77%	LOWER LEG	55%		MAXIMUM RANGE	
UPPER ARM	61%				475m	
ZOOM	2X				WEIGHT	
MUZZLE FLASH SCALE	2.0				4.75kg	
MAGAZINE CAPACITY	30 ROUNDS					

This is a sample of the M16A2's Accuracy Table.

KILL POWER

The weapons in Ghost Recon are powerful, but not always lethal on the first shot. There are actually seven different places you can wound an enemy in Ghost Recon, each with a different chance of slaying them outright. The hit locations are Head, Chest, Abdomen, Upper Arm, Lower Arm, Upper Leg, and Lower Leg. A shot to the Lower Arm can be lethal (severing a main artery for example) but shooting someone in the Head has a much higher chance of slaying them outright. Whenever a character is shot, the game calculates whether or not they are killed outright or simply take a wound based on the gun's Kill Power, how far away the target is from the shooter, and where the shot strikes. The formula is actually a little complex, so a table has been created for each gun to show the percent chance the gun has of slaying an enemy if it

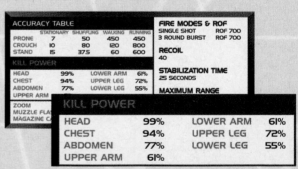

hits in the listed hit location at a range of 100 m. The sample is of the M16A2's Kill Power. As you can see, at 100 m the M16A2 has a high chance of killing a target in a single shot in nearly every hit location except the Lower Arm and Leg. Head shots, regardless of range, are almost always instantly lethal.

ACCURACY TABLE	STATIONARY	SHUFFLING	WALKING	RUNNING	FIRE MODES & ROF	
PRONE	7	50	450	450	SINGLE SHOT	ROF 700
CROUCH	10	80	120	800	3 ROUND BURST	ROF 700
STAND	15	37.5	60	600	RECOIL	
KILL POWER					40	
HEAD	99%	LOWER ARM	61%		STABILIZATION TIME	
CHEST	94%	UPPER LEG	72%		25 SECONDS	
ABDOMEN	77%	LOWER LEG	55%		MAXIMUM RANGE	
UPPER ARM						

KILL POWER			
HEAD	99%	LOWER ARM	61%
CHEST	94%	UPPER LEG	72%
ABDOMEN	77%	LOWER LEG	55%
UPPER ARM	61%		

ACCURACY TABLE			
	STATIONARY	SHUFFLING	WALKING	RUNNING
PRONE	7	50	450	450
CROUCH	10	80	120	800
STAND	15	37.5	60	600

KILL POWER
HEAD
CHEST
ABDOMEN
UPPER ARM
ZOOM
MUZZLE FLASH
MAGAZINE CAPACITY 30 ROUNDS

FIRE MODES & ROF
SINGLE SHOT ROF 700
3 ROUND BURST ROF 700

RECOIL
40

STABILIZATION TIME

ZOOM	2X
MUZZLE FLASH SCALE	2.0
MAGAZINE CAPACITY	30 ROUNDS

4.75kg

ZOOM LEVELS

Most guns in Ghost Recon come equipped with some kind of scope or sight. The power of these scopes varies from gun to gun, with sniper rifles having the most zoom power and pistols having none at all. The farther a gun can zoom, the easier it is to hit a target at longer ranges. Zoom levels are listed in their order of magnitude; 10x zoom means 10 times normal magnification.

MUZZLE FLASH SCALE

When a gun fires, the explosion that launches the bullet releases a small amount of bright light from the gun's barrel. This is commonly referred to as muzzle flash, and each gun in Ghost Recon has a different amount of muzzle flash. In practical terms, the higher a gun's muzzle flash number, the easier it is to see from longer distances, and the harder it will be for its firer to remain hidden while firing. If a weapon is silenced, it has almost no muzzle flash, and enemies will generally not be able to detect where the shots are coming from unless you are extremely close or miss consecutive shots near the enemy.

FIRE MODES & RATE OF FIRE

There are three types of fire modes a gun can be set to: single-shot, 3-round burst, or fully automatic. Some guns do not have all three modes; Sniper rifles are single-shot only, and most machine guns are full auto only. Additionally, each gun can fire a different maximum number of rounds per minute, assuming that it has unlimited ammo. The higher a gun's Rate of Fire, the more theoretical bullets it can fire per minute.

RECOIL & STABILIZATION TIME

When fired, a gun produces a certain amount of kickback to the shooter. Typically, the more powerful the gun, the more recoil it has. In Ghost Recon, the higher a gun's recoil value, the more it kicks back. Similarly, the higher the stabilization time, the longer it takes for the shooter to stabilize the gun after each shot.

MAXIMUM RANGE

When a bullet leaves a gun's barrel, gravity slowly drags it to the ground. The distance a bullet can cover before

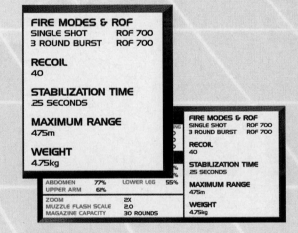

FIRE MODES & ROF
SINGLE SHOT ROF 700
3 ROUND BURST ROF 700

RECOIL
40

STABILIZATION TIME
.25 SECONDS

MAXIMUM RANGE
475m

WEIGHT
4.75kg

| ABDOMEN | 77% | LOWER LEG | 55% |
| UPPER ARM | 61% | | |

ZOOM	2X
MUZZLE FLASH SCALE	2.0
MAGAZINE CAPACITY	30 ROUNDS

FIRE MODES & ROF
SINGLE SHOT ROF 700
3 ROUND BURST ROF 700

RECOIL
40

STABILIZATION TIME
.25 SECONDS

MAXIMUM RANGE
475m

WEIGHT
4.75kg

it has fallen 2 m is listed as the gun's maximum range in Ghost Recon. For most rifles and large guns, you can shoot much farther than you can see, but for some of the smaller weapons, you may be unable to hit a distant target because its range exceeds your gun's maximum effective range.

WEIGHT

The more a gun weighs, the slower you move with it.

WEAPONRY & EQUIPMENT

Assault Rifles

The Riflemen are the exclusive users of the assault rifles. They are probably the most balanced weapons in the game—a strong combination of range, firepower, and accuracy. They are probably the most useful multiplayer weapons as well, especially in a free-for-all deathmatch-style game.

Carbines

The carbines in Ghost Recon are supposed to be slightly less potent than the assault rifles, but in practice they are just as lethal. Only the Demolitions class uses carbines. Both carbines are just as versatile and powerful as the two assault rifles, making them excellent multiplayer weapons. In fact, the carbines are a little more accurate while moving, meaning they may even be superior to the assault rifles in multiplayer, where speed matters significantly.

Light Machine Guns

Unlike most of the other weapons in Ghost Recon, the light machine guns (LMG) are designed to fire in full auto. Only Support soldiers have access to the LMGs, and they're a mixed bag in terms of usefulness. Overall, the LMGs are not as accurate as the assault rifles and carbines, but they have a lower recoil penalty after each shot. LMGs are mainly defensive weapons; if

you try to use them offensively, you'll quickly discover that even their capacity for sustained automatic fire doesn't compensate for their accuracy problems. Keep your Support soldiers out of the front lines and try to lead the enemy to them. LMGs work best while prone, so try to get your Support soldiers prone before firing. Due to their defensive nature, support weapons aren't that useful in multiplayer matches, unless you are working with a coordinated team which can buy time for the Support soldier to get his heavy gun in a useful position.

Pistols

There is only a handful of situations where pistols are useful in Ghost Recon, but they do have some purpose. Unlike every other gun in the game, pistols are always secondary weapons. For characters armed with long-range weapons only, a pistol can provide some close-range fire support.

Sniper Rifles

The kings of long-range combat are the sniper rifles. With a large zoom, a high kill power, huge recoil and muzzle flash, they are used for long-range combat almost exclusively. Additionally, most sniper rifles are not meant for repetitive fire, so trying to mow down a charging squad of soldiers before they reach your position can be quite difficult,

depending on the range. Sniper rifles also don't handle movement well; you must slowly train your crosshairs on an enemy, or your weapon pips will disperse quite a distance. Sniper rifles are the long arms of the law, but if you can slip inside their reach, they lose a lot of their effectiveness.

Submachine Guns

While most other guns are class-specific, both the Demolition and Rifleman classes use the submachine guns. The two submachine guns are sort of a mesh between a pistol and a carbine. While they both boast a high rate of fire, neither is really potent long-range weapon. Since these are primary weapons, it is almost a prerequisite that their wielders have a high Stealth.

EXPLOSIVES

Explosives have slightly different entries than do the guns. The Kill Power tables have been modified to show a victim's chance of being killed when 5 m from the center of the explosion. Additionally, the hand grenades and Claymores don't have an Accuracy Table due to their special firing natures. Tactically speaking, the explosives in Ghost Recon work as indirect fire weapons or as group dispersion weapons. If the enemy is camping in a specific spot, hurling a few grenades or rockets into their midst will force them to scatter or suffer multiple casualties. Explosive weapons can also attack enemies you can't see, so they're a bit more devious than standard guns. Most of the explosives in Ghost Recon are support weapons rather than primary weapons; learn the few situations in which they're more potent than guns and use them appropriately.

EXTRA EQUIPMENT

AN / GVS-5 Binoculars

If you want to give your troops a little extra zooming power, and you don't have a Sniper nearby, you can equip them with binoculars. The binoculars allow you to zoom in up to 2X magnification,  and they have a sort of rangefinder capability when placed on a target, but they're not as useful as many of the other secondary weapons. 2X magnification isn't any better than the scope on almost *any* weapon, so it's really not recommended to use the binoculars at all.

AN/GSQ-187 Sensor

Another oddity in the Ghost Recon arsenal is the portable sensor. While it doesn't actually attack your enemies, once placed it will reveal every nearby enemy's presence on your Command map. It has a 40m detection range, just like the red center of your Threat Indicator. One of the special advantages of the sensor is that it can detect enemies through any kind of terrain—even solid walls! This allows you to spot and locate enemies in buildings. In single-player, this can let you preemptively scout out a building before entering, or you can place it on your flank to make sure that no enemies sneak up behind your fireteam. In multiplayer, especially when Threat Indicators are turned off, the sensor can be a big help in ferreting out a hidden foe. In a team multiplayer environment, these can be invaluable in ensuring that your team's flank is secure.

M2 Demolitions Charge

You only need the M2 demolitions charge for certain single-player objectives, and it has no combat potential, so its entry here will be short. One slight note: if you command a squad that is armed  with M2 charges to move near a mission objective that is flagged to be destroyed, your troops will automatically place a charge on it. This can be good or bad, depending on whether or not you wanted them to put the charge down.

M16A2

STATS WITH M203 GL ATTACHED

ACCURACY TABLE

	STATIONARY	SHUFFLING	WALKING	RUNNING
PRONE	7	50	450	450
CROUCH	10	80	120	800
STAND	15	37.5	60	600

KILL POWER

HEAD	99%	LOWER ARM	44%
CHEST	94%	UPPER LEG	72%
ABDOMEN	77%	LOWER LEG	55%
UPPER ARM	61%		

ZOOM	2X
MUZZLE FLASH SCALE	2.0
MAGAZINE CAPACITY	30 ROUNDS

FIRE MODES & ROF

SINGLE SHOT	ROF 700
3 ROUND BURST	ROF 700

RECOIL
40

STABILIZATION TIME
.25 SECONDS

MAXIMUM RANGE
475 m

WEIGHT
4.76 kg

M16A2

If there's one weapon that serves as the default weapon for all other measurements in Ghost Recon, it's the M16A2. Perhaps the only really mentionable feature of the M16A2 is its lack of a fully automatic fire mode. While early models of the M16 were capable of fully automatic fire, the A2 model was changed to fire only 3-round bursts in order to conserve ammunition. The M16A2 is a fairly universal weapon, with enough firepower and effective range to be useful in nearly every role. Additionally, the M16A2 is capable of being fitted with the M203 Underbarrel Grenade Launcher, which is covered in the Explosives section of this chapter. There are some differences between using the M16 standalone and the M16/M203 combination. The extra weight and encumbrance of the M203 Grenade Launcher makes the M16 a little less accurate. While it's not a huge penalty, if you find yourself not using the M203, you may want to use a different secondary weapon to avoid the penalty. All standard Riflemen soldiers use the M16 as their primary weapon.

ACCURACY TABLE

	STATIONARY	SHUFFLING	WALKING	RUNNING
PRONE	5	45	400	400
CROUCH	8	60	100	750
STAND	10	80	50	500

KILL POWER

HEAD	99%	LOWER ARM	44%
CHEST	94%	UPPER LEG	72%
ABDOMEN	77%	LOWER LEG	55%
UPPER ARM	61%		

ZOOM	2X
MUZZLE FLASH SCALE	2.0
MAGAZINE CAPACITY	30 ROUNDS

FIRE MODES & ROF

SINGLE SHOT	ROF 700
3 ROUND BURST	ROF 700

RECOIL
50

STABILIZATION TIME
.2 SECONDS

MAXIMUM RANGE
475 m

WEIGHT
3.4 kg

OICW

STATS FOR OICW/GL COMBO WEAPON

ACCURACY TABLE

	STATIONARY	SHUFFLING	WALKING	RUNNING
PRONE	4	45	350	350
CROUCH	8	55	200	900
STAND	10	35	60	600

KILL POWER

HEAD	99%	LOWER ARM	44%
CHEST	94%	UPPER LEG	72%
ABDOMEN	77%	LOWER LEG	55%
UPPER ARM	61%		

ZOOM	3X
MUZZLE FLASH SCALE	1.5
MAGAZINE CAPACITY	30 ROUNDS

FIRE MODES & ROF

SINGLE SHOT	ROF 750
3 ROUND BURST	ROF 750
FULL AUTO	ROF 775

RECOIL
42

STABILIZATION TIME
.2 SECONDS

MAXIMUM RANGE
475 m

WEIGHT
5 kg

OICW

One of the military's more modern weapons, still in testing stages, is the Objective Individual Combat Weapon (OICW). This weapon is unique in that its base configuration is a combo high-powered assault rifle with an overbarrel 20mm grenade launcher. In game terms, the OICW comes in two varieties. You can either take the combo weapon itself (which occupies both your primary and secondary weapon slots), or just the rifle portion and a different secondary weapon. When using the combo weapon, the OICW assault rifle is a little less accurate than the M16/M203 combination. However, it has a slightly higher ROF, a better zoom, less recoil, and less muzzle flash than an M16. If you choose to use just the rifle portion of the OICW, it is very roughly comparable to the standalone M16. The M16 is still a little more accurate, but the OICW has a much better zoom and a higher ROF. While it's not really much of an advantage, the OICW is also capable of fully automatic fire. The OICW GL greatly outclasses the M203; you can read more on that in the Explosives section of this chapter. Will Jacobs and Lindy Cohen, two Riflemen specialists, are the only characters that use the OICW in the single player campaign.

ACCURACY TABLE

	STATIONARY	SHUFFLING	WALKING	RUNNING
PRONE	3	45	300	300
CROUCH	5	50	175	800
STAND	8	32	48	560

KILL POWER

HEAD	99%	LOWER ARM	44%
CHEST	94%	UPPER LEG	72%
ABDOMEN	77%	LOWER LEG	55%
UPPER ARM	61%		

ZOOM	5X
MUZZLE FLASH SCALE	1.5
MAGAZINE CAPACITY	30 ROUNDS

FIRE MODES & ROF

SINGLE SHOT	ROF 750
3 ROUND BURST	ROF 750
FULL AUTO	ROF 775

RECOIL
50

STABILIZATION TIME
.175 SECONDS

MAXIMUM RANGE
475 m

WEIGHT
5 kg

M4

If not for the fact that the M16 is more accurate while motionless (important for long range firing), the M4 would actually outclass it completely. The M4 is an "M16 light;" it has the exact same kill power and range of the M16, but it weighs less. This makes the gun more useful while on the move, but it does have a bit more recoil and lower maximum accuracy. The M4 can't fire in 3-round bursts like the M16, so be careful about going crazy with the fully automatic setting. The M4 is the default weapon carried by all regular Demolitions soldiers.

ACCURACY TABLE

	STATIONARY	SHUFFLING	WALKING	RUNNING
PRONE	8	65	250	250
CROUCH	10	80	110	650
STAND	15	45	60	525

KILL POWER

HEAD	99%	LOWER ARM	44%
CHEST	94%	UPPER LEG	72%
ABDOMEN	77%	LOWER LEG	55%
UPPER ARM	61%		

ZOOM	2X
MUZZLE FLASH SCALE	1.5
MAGAZINE CAPACITY	30 ROUNDS

FIRE MODES & ROF

SINGLE SHOT	ROF 750
FULL AUTO	ROF 750

RECOIL
53

STABILIZATION TIME
.15 SECONDS

MAXIMUM RANGE
475 m

WEIGHT
2.54 kg

GUNS - CARBINES

SA-80

Compared to the M4 and the M16, the SA80 sits about in the middle. The SA80 is heavier and a little more unwieldy on the move than the M4, but it is still easier to use while running than the M16. The SA80 also sports a slightly higher ROF than the M4 and has a slightly lower stabilization time. Its main draw, however, is that the SA80 has a 3x zoom, whereas the M16 and M4 are only 2x zoom weapons. However, the SA80 is still a carbine weapon, so even though it can zoom farther out than the M16, it does not have as high a maximum accuracy as the M16. The SA80 isn't clearly superior to the M4; it's more a matter of preference. Demolitions specialist Nigel Tunney is the only character in the single player campaign to use the SA80.

GUNS - CARBINES

ACCURACY TABLE

	STATIONARY	SHUFFLING	WALKING	RUNNING
PRONE	8	55	300	300
CROUCH	10	65	120	750
STAND	15	45	60	525

KILL POWER

HEAD	99%	LOWER ARM	44%
CHEST	94%	UPPER LEG	72%
ABDOMEN	77%	LOWER LEG	55%
UPPER ARM	61%		

ZOOM	3X
MUZZLE FLASH SCALE	1.5
MAGAZINE CAPACITY	30 ROUNDS

FIRE MODES & ROF

SINGLE SHOT	ROF 775
FULL AUTO	ROF 775

RECOIL
53

STABILIZATION TIME
.125 SECONDS

MAXIMUM RANGE
475 m

WEIGHT
3.71 kg

M249 SAW

STATS FOR M249 SAW

When compared to the default M16, the M249 Squad Automatic Weapon has a few things about it that unfortunately make it a bit impractical. The M249 is unwieldy while moving, has a large muzzle flash, and does not boast an especially high rate of fire. However, it does have a gigantic magazine capacity—almost seven times that of the M16—making it useful for extended suppression. It all practicality however, it is unlikely that you'll ever manage to run through all 200 rounds unless you are fending off a much larger group of enemies. All your default Support soldiers are equipped with the M249 SAW.

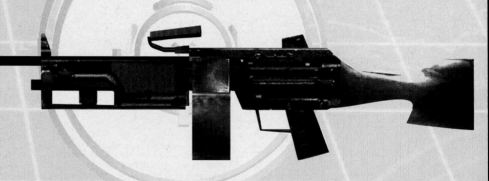

ACCURACY TABLE

	STATIONARY	SHUFFLING	WALKING	RUNNING
PRONE	5	70	500	500
CROUCH	20	80	300	1200
STAND	40	60	240	1000

KILL POWER

HEAD	99%	LOWER ARM	44%
CHEST	94%	UPPER LEG	72%
ABDOMEN	77%	LOWER LEG	55%
UPPER ARM	61%		

ZOOM	2X
MUZZLE FLASH SCALE	2.5
MAGAZINE CAPACITY	200 ROUNDS

FIRE MODES & ROF
FULL AUTO   ROF 750

RECOIL
40

STABILIZATION TIME
.25 SECONDS

MAXIMUM RANGE
475 m

WEIGHT
7.03 kg

MG3

Every game needs a gigantic, overpowered gun, and in Ghost Recon the MG3 is that gun. The MG3 weighs a staggering 11 kg, and is horribly inaccurate if the wielder is moving at all. Additionally, the MG3 has a huge muzzle flash, making it nearly impossible to hide while using it. However, the MG3 boasts an unmatched rate of fire, and its rounds have roughly a 10% greater chance to kill than that of the M249 or M16. The MG3 truly epitomizes the defensive nature of the support weapons. If you have a soldier equipped with the MG3, get him into a spot with good defensive cover and let him hose any enemies who are unlucky enough to move within his range. Dieter Munz, the last specialist in the game, is the only soldier who uses the MG3 in the single-player campaign.

ACCURACY TABLE

	STATIONARY	SHUFFLING	WALKING	RUNNING
PRONE	5	75	300	300
CROUCH	15	80	275	1600
STAND	25	56	245	1400

KILL POWER

HEAD	99%	LOWER ARM	56%
CHEST	95%	UPPER LEG	78%
ABDOMEN	82%	LOWER LEG	65%
UPPER ARM	69%		

ZOOM	2X
MUZZLE FLASH SCALE	3.0
MAGAZINE CAPACITY	100 ROUNDS

FIRE MODES & ROF
FULL AUTO   ROF 1300

RECOIL
30

STABILIZATION TIME
.25 SECONDS

MAXIMUM RANGE
475 m

WEIGHT
11.05 kg

RPK74

STATS FOR RPK74

The RPK74 is much more like an assault rifle than the other two support weapons. It is actually a modified version of the AK74 assault rifle, so the similarity to assault rifles is not coincidental. Not only is the RPK74 more stable while moving than any other support weapon, but it is also the only support weapon capable of firing in single-shot mode. However, in order to make it more mobile, the RPK74 had to sacrifice both hitting power and ammunition capacity. It's hard to decide whether the RPK74 is a successful hybrid of assault rifle and light machine gun or a useless combination that shares the worst features of each. Either way, it occupies a unique position in the weapon scheme of Ghost Recon. The Russian Support specialist Guram Osadze is the sole user of the RPK74 in the single-player campaign.

ACCURACY TABLE

	STATIONARY	SHUFFLING	WALKING	RUNNING
PRONE	5	60	450	450
CROUCH	20	90	250	1100
STAND	40	50	200	900

KILL POWER

HEAD	99%	LOWER ARM	41%
CHEST	94%	UPPER LEG	70%
ABDOMEN	76%	LOWER LEG	52%
UPPER ARM	58%		

ZOOM	2X
MUZZLE FLASH SCALE	2.75
MAGAZINE CAPACITY	75 ROUNDS

FIRE MODES & ROF

SINGLE SHOT	ROF 660
FULL AUTO	ROF 660

RECOIL
43

STABILIZATION TIME
.25 SECONDS

MAXIMUM RANGE
475 m

WEIGHT
5.0 kg

M9

STATS FOR M9

As you can tell by its Kill Power table, the M9 Pistol isn't that deadly a weapon at 100 m. It is not really designed to be used beyond about 50 m or so, though, so this really isn't much of a concern. At point blank range the M9 sports a decent fire rate and enough firepower to kill an enemy if you manage to shoot him in the head or chest. Additionally, the gun has a low muzzle flash, and is very movement friendly. The combination of the two makes this gun at least modestly useful for indoor combat. Only Snipers bother to use the non-silenced version of this gun; they lack close-range firepower so they may actually wish to use the M9 instead of the M9-SD.

GUNS - PISTOLS

ACCURACY TABLE

	STATIONARY	SHUFFLING	WALKING	RUNNING
PRONE	10	50	200	200
CROUCH	15	65	150	650
STAND	30	60	70	600

KILL POWER

HEAD	97%	LOWER ARM	0%
CHEST	73%	UPPER LEG	0%
ABDOMEN	0%	LOWER LEG	0%
UPPER ARM	0%		

ZOOM	IX
MUZZLE FLASH SCALE	1.0
MAGAZINE CAPACITY	15 ROUNDS

FIRE MODES & ROF
SINGLE SHOT   ROF 600

RECOIL
100

STABILIZATION TIME
.25 SECONDS

MAXIMUM RANGE
246 m

WEIGHT
0.95 kg

M9-SD

STATS FOR M9-SD

Nearly every class and every specialist has the option of carrying the M9-SD, so they can have at least one silenced weapon when needed. The M9-SD has the same tactical uses as the M9, except it is also silenced. The addition of the silencer makes the gun easier to control while running, but it further hampers the gun's already low kill power. If you're not overly concerned with being quiet, you might as well take the M9. Since you'll have to be at fairly close range to use a pistol, it's unlikely that the enemy won't already have detected your presence.

GUNS - PISTOLS

ACCURACY TABLE

	STATIONARY	SHUFFLING	WALKING	RUNNING
PRONE	10	55	200	200
CROUCH	12	70	180	550
STAND	25	50	75	300

KILL POWER

HEAD	96%	LOWER ARM	0%
CHEST	61%	UPPER LEG	0%
ABDOMEN	0%	LOWER LEG	0%
UPPER ARM	0%		

ZOOM	IX
MUZZLE FLASH SCALE	.01 (SILENCED)
MAGAZINE CAPACITY	15 ROUNDS

FIRE MODES & ROF
SINGLE SHOT   ROF 600

RECOIL
90

STABILIZATION TIME
.275 SECONDS

MAXIMUM RANGE
246 m

WEIGHT
1.11 kg

M24

It's hard to find anything special about the M24, because it's not really quite as advanced as the other sniper rifles. While it does have the highest maximum accuracy of any sniper rifle, it also has the smallest clip and the least powerful zoom. If you want a more mobile sniper rifle, the L96A1 is a better deal overall. If you want a heavier and longer-range sniper rifle, the M82A1 and SVD are both better than the M24. The M24 is a bolt-action sniper rifle as well, further reducing its overall appeal. Your default Snipers in the single player campaign are all equipped with M24 sniper rifles.

ACCURACY TABLE

	STATIONARY	SHUFFLING	WALKING	RUNNING
PRONE	.5	70	600	600
CROUCH	1	95	300	1500
STAND	2	46	120	1000

KILL POWER

HEAD	99%	LOWER ARM	56%
CHEST	95%	UPPER LEG	78%
ABDOMEN	82%	LOWER LEG	65%
UPPER ARM	69%		

ZOOM	5X
MUZZLE FLASH SCALE	3.0
MAGAZINE CAPACITY	6 ROUNDS

FIRE MODES & ROF
SINGLE SHOT   ROF 300

RECOIL
100

STABILIZATION TIME
.45 SECONDS

MAXIMUM RANGE
475 m

WEIGHT
6.284 kg

M82AI

With a combination of firepower and range, the M82A1 sits in the middle of the sniper rifle hierarchy. It is incredibly heavy—even heavier than the support weapons. The M82A1 also has a gigantic muzzle flash; fortunately it has a nice 10x zoom to help make sure that you can stay far away from the enemy while using it. While it is not as walk- or run-friendly as the L96A1 or M24, shuffle movement does not affect the M82A1

as much as it does the other sniper rifles. The M82A1 doesn't have quite the reach of the SVD, but it packs a gigantic punch and is semi-automatic. If you're not terribly worried about the heavy or noisy nature of the gun, the M82A1 can be a lot of fun. Scott Ibrahim, one of the last specialists you unlock, is the only soldier who wields a M82A1 in the single-player campaign.

ACCURACY TABLE

	STATIONARY	SHUFFLING	WALKING	RUNNING
PRONE	.5	20	300	300
CROUCH	2	60	200	1800
STAND	5	50	125	1500

KILL POWER

HEAD	99%	LOWER ARM	62%
CHEST	96%	UPPER LEG	81%
ABDOMEN	84%	LOWER LEG	69%
UPPER ARM	73%		

ZOOM	5X, 10X
MUZZLE FLASH SCALE	4.0
MAGAZINE CAPACITY	10 ROUNDS

FIRE MODES & ROF
SINGLE SHOT   ROF 300

RECOIL
100

STABILIZATION TIME
.65 SECONDS

MAXIMUM RANGE
481 m

WEIGHT
12.9 kg

L96A1

STATS FOR L96A1

It's not as accurate as the M24, and it's also the weakest sniper rifle in the game, but the L96A1 is fairly movement-friendly, is relatively quiet, and has a low recoil and stabilization time. The L96A1 is a bolt-action sniper rifle, but it has a larger magazine than the M24. If you don't want to be tied down by the heavier sniper rifles, and you're not very fond of the M24 with its small clip and 5x zoom, the L96A1 is a great sniper rifle. The first Sniper specialist you unlock, Jack Stone, is the only soldier who comes equipped with a L96A1 in the single-player campaign.

GUNS - SNIPER RIFLES

ACCURACY TABLE

	STATIONARY	SHUFFLING	WALKING	RUNNING
PRONE	.75	70	500	600
CROUCH	2	90	200	1200
STAND	5	45	125	1000

KILL POWER

HEAD	99%	LOWER ARM	44%
CHEST	94%	UPPER LEG	72%
ABDOMEN	77%	LOWER LEG	55%
UPPER ARM	61%		

ZOOM	6X
MUZZLE FLASH SCALE	2.5
MAGAZINE CAPACITY	10 ROUNDS

FIRE MODES & ROF
SINGLE SHOT   ROF 300

RECOIL
75

STABILIZATION TIME
.5 SECONDS

MAXIMUM RANGE
475 m

WEIGHT
3.4 kg

SVD 'DRAGUNOV'

STATS FOR SVD 'DRAGUNOV'

If you want to reach out and touch someone from half a kilometer away, the SVD is the perfect gun. Unfortunately, this reach comes at a price. The SVD is horribly, grossly, inaccurate while running. The gun must be used from the crouching or prone stance to be very effective. The second zoom on the SVD goes out to an amazing 15X, allowing you to make pinpoint shots on pretty much any enemy that can be seen. As long as you can keep your SVD-wielding Sniper away from the front lines of combat, they can be quite a force to be reckoned with. The SVD is semi-automatic like the M82A1, but it has the large recoil penalty; don't expect to be able to sustain rapid accurate fire. The middle Sniper specialist, Astra Galinsky, comes equipped with the SVD Dragunov.

ACCURACY TABLE

	STATIONARY	SHUFFLING	WALKING	RUNNING
PRONE	1	50	350	350
CROUCH	5	140	400	3500
STAND	10	120	310	3000

KILL POWER

HEAD	99%	LOWER ARM	56%
CHEST	95%	UPPER LEG	78%
ABDOMEN	82%	LOWER LEG	65%
UPPER ARM	69%		

ZOOM	5X, 15X
MUZZLE FLASH SCALE	3.0
MAGAZINE CAPACITY	10 ROUNDS

FIRE MODES & ROF
SINGLE SHOT   ROF 300

RECOIL
110

STABILIZATION TIME
.4 SECONDS

MAXIMUM RANGE
500m

WEIGHT
4.3 kg

MP5

The first model of submachine gun acts more like a rapid-fire pistol than an assault rifle. The MP5 is modestly potent at short ranges, but it is definitely not a good gun to use in a long-range firefight. The MP5 works fairly well from the standing stance, perfect for frantic indoor combat. If you have an option between the MP5 and the MP5-SD, the MP5-SD is almost always the better bet. Klaus Henkel, the final Demolitions specialist you unlock, comes equipped with the standard MP5.

GUNS - SUBMACHINE GUNS

ACCURACY TABLE

	STATIONARY	SHUFFLING	WALKING	RUNNING
PRONE	8	55	200	200
CROUCH	15	70	180	550
STAND	25	50	75	300

KILL POWER

HEAD	96%	LOWER ARM	0%
CHEST	61%	UPPER LEG	0%
ABDOMEN	0%	LOWER LEG	0%
UPPER ARM	0%		

ZOOM	1.5X
MUZZLE FLASH SCALE	1.0
MAGAZINE CAPACITY	30 ROUNDS

FIRE MODES & ROF

SINGLE SHOT	ROF 800
3 ROUND BURST	ROF 800
FULL AUTO	ROF 800

RECOIL
53

STABILIZATION TIME
.125 SECONDS

MAXIMUM RANGE
220 m

WEIGHT
2.54 kg

MP5-SD

STATS FOR MP5-SD

While the MP5 may only be a short-range weapon, its silenced counterpart, the MP5-SD, has much more potent long-range capabilities. The lack of a significant zoom hampers the MP5-SD's sniping capabilities, but it does not suffer from the same massive drop-off in bullet killing power that the MP5 does at long ranges. Most notable about this gun, however, is its silencer. The combination of modest range capabilities plus a silencer makes this gun an awesome assassination and sneak-attack gun. If equipped on a soldier with a high Stealth stat, you can easily ambush a group of enemies from 50–100 m out and mow them all down before they ever spot you. The MP5-SD works well in the standing stance as well, making it a fairly versatile weapon overall. Two specialists, the Rifleman Henry Ramirez and the Demolitions specialist Susan Grey, both come equipped with the MP5-SD.

ACCURACY TABLE

	STATIONARY	SHUFFLING	WALKING	RUNNING
PRONE	8	50	350	350
CROUCH	10	60	200	650
STAND	20	40	60	400

KILL POWER

HEAD	99%	LOWER ARM	44%
CHEST	94%	UPPER LEG	72%
ABDOMEN	77%	LOWER LEG	55%
UPPER ARM	61%		

ZOOM	1.5X
MUZZLE FLASH SCALE	0.01 (SILENCED)
MAGAZINE CAPACITY	30 ROUNDS

FIRE MODES & ROF

SINGLE SHOT	ROF 700
3 ROUND BURST	ROF 700
FULL AUTO	ROF 700

RECOIL
50

STABILIZATION TIME
.15 SECONDS

MAXIMUM RANGE
475 m

WEIGHT
3.4 kg

M136

ANTI-TANK ROCKET LAUNCHER

The M136 is designed to be used against tanks, but it can be used against infantry in a pinch. The rockets have a pretty hefty 10m blast radius, but the rocket launcher itself is very slow to aim. In order to get the launcher to fire, you must remain motionless and allow the pips to converge to their minimum setting. This limits using the M136 offensively to mainly sneak attacks, but it can still be used defensively quite effectively. If an M136 hits in the middle of a group, it stands a good chance of wiping out the entire fireteam. In the single-player campaign, you'll use your M136s against a variety of enemy tanks. When attacking an enemy tank, you must stay out of the tank's line of sight or it will rip you apart with its heavy machine gun. Additionally, the M136 has no zoom feature, so you'll have to line up any long-range rocket attacks with a different weapon and then switch over to your M136.

ACCURACY TABLE

	STATIONARY	SHUFFLING	WALKING	RUNNING
PRONE	1.5	50	300	300
CROUCH	2	60	150	700
STAND	4	40	100	500

KILL POWER

HEAD	99%	LOWER ARM	54%
CHEST	95%	UPPER LEG	77%
ABDOMEN	81%	LOWER LEG	63%
UPPER ARM	67%		

ZOOM		IX
MUZZLE FLASH SCALE		1.0
MAGAZINE CAPACITY		1 ROUND

FIRE MODES & ROF
SINGLE SHOT   ROF 600

BLAST RADIUS
10 m

RECOIL
1.5

STABILIZATION TIME
1 SECOND

MAXIMUM RANGE
188 m

EXPLOSIVES

MI8

CLAYMORE MINE

There really isn't any other weapon in the game quite like the Claymore Mine. Unlike a grenade or rocket that is thrown or launched, the Claymore Mine is planted in the ground and then later detonated manually by the original wielder. When the mine explodes, it fans out, creating a conical explosion. The cone is directed out in the same direction as the deployer was facing when he placed the mine. At its maximum length, the forward cone is 25 m long and 45 m in width. There is a smaller backwards cone, extending 5 m back at 7.5 m in width. Obviously, this is a very large explosion. Getting a Claymore into position and managing to trick someone into walking into its blast radius is the hard part. You're going to need to plant the Claymore in a position that you suspect or know the enemy will need to move through, so any tactical choke points or defensive positions are prime locations for the Claymore. In the single-player campaign, you can place a Claymore mine and then use your other troops to

create a distraction and lead the enemy into the mine's path. In multiplayer, if you are playing on a team, the concept works the same. The Claymore Mine is mainly a team weapon; unless you're very patient and persistent, it doesn't do well in a free-for-all deathmatch environment.

BLAST RADIUS

SPECIAL

KILL POWER

HEAD	99%
CHEST	99%
ABDOMEN	97%
UPPER ARM	95%
LOWER ARM	93%
LOWER LEG	96%
UPPER LEG	94%

M203

UNDERBARREL GRENADE LAUNCHER

The Rifleman class has exclusive access to the M203. The M203 is attached underneath an M16 and functions as a single-shot grenade launcher. The blast is modestly powerful and has a fair bit more practical range than a regular hand grenade. Unlike hand grenades, the M203 round explodes on impact. This means that you can't bounce the grenade around corners or off walls, but instead you can use it to hit things like trees and walls near enemies to cause a mid-air detonation of the grenade. The M203 makes a nice room-sweeping weapon if you need to invade a building. Have someone open the door and then a Rifleman can pop by and launch a round into the room.

ACCURACY TABLE

	STATIONARY	SHUFFLING	WALKING	RUNNING
PRONE	7	50	450	450
CROUCH	10	80	120	800
STAND	15	37.5	60	600

KILL POWER

HEAD	98%	LOWER ARM	0%
CHEST	88%	UPPER LEG	44%
ABDOMEN	55%	LOWER LEG	11%
UPPER ARM	22%		

ZOOM	IX
MUZZLE FLASH SCALE	0.0
MAGAZINE CAPACITY	1 ROUND

FIRE MODES & ROF
SINGLE SHOT　　　　ROF 600

BLAST RADIUS
8 M

RECOIL
1.5

STABILIZATION TIME
.25 SECONDS

M67

HAND GRENADE

Another unique tool in the Ghost Recon arsenal is the M67 Hand Grenade. The M67 grenades are actually thrown, instead of fired like every other grenade in the game. This obviously limits the effective range of the grenade, but it allows you to arc it into the air and over impeding terrain. The grenade does not detonate on impact; it detonates after a preset 4-second delay. This gives you a little tactical flexibility, allowing you to bounce it off walls and other objects, but it makes it impractical to stop a charge. If you pull out a hand grenade and the enemy pulls out a pistol, you're going to lose. You can use the M67 as a trap weapon. If you know an enemy is approaching your position, you can draw his attention, drop the grenade a little in front of yourself, then pull back and hope the enemy accidentally walks into the blast radius. It takes some practice and patience to get used to the arc and range of the M67, but it can be a useful tool in both single and multiplayer if you work at it.

BLAST RADIUS

10 m (4 SECOND DELAY)

KILL POWER

HEAD	99%
CHEST	95%
ABDOMEN	81%
UPPER ARM	67%
LOWER ARM	54%
LOWER LEG	77%
UPPER LEG	63%

OICW

When equipped with an OICW, the default configuration is to take the OICW grenade launcher as well. The main difference between the OICW grenade launcher and the M203 is that the OICW is a clip-fed, semi-automatic grenade launcher. The M203 fires larger, more powerful grenades, but the OICW can more than make up for in volume what the M203 has in power. While it may not be as fast as a machine gun, the OICW grenade launcher can fire fast enough to create a rather large death zone by spamming all six of its grenades in a matter of one or two seconds. This makes the OICW grenade launcher a very potent tool for disrupting large groups of enemy soldiers. In the single-player campaign, this makes a lot of commotion and can be counter-productive if overused, but it is very potent in multiplayer matches. By using the Threat Indicator to guesstimate the direction and location of your opponents, you don't even have to see them in order to lay down a field of explosions on top of them.

EXPLOSIVES

ACCURACY TABLE

	STATIONARY	SHUFFLING	WALKING	RUNNING
PRONE	4	45	350	350
CROUCH	8	55	200	900
STAND	10	35	600	650

KILL POWER

HEAD	98%	LOWER ARM	0%
CHEST	81%	UPPER LEG	7%
ABDOMEN	26%	LOWER LEG	0%
UPPER ARM	0%		

ZOOM	IX
MUZZLE FLASH SCALE	0.00001
MAGAZINE CAPACITY	6 ROUNDS

FIRE MODES & ROF
SINGLE SHOT   ROF 600

BLAST RADIUS
7 m

RECOIL
1.5

STABILIZATION TIME
1 SECOND

CHAPTER 4
Tactics and Strategies

CHAPTER 4
Tactics and Strategies

Rushing forth into the fray, guns blazing, typically ensures a quick defeat in Ghost Recon. Careful positioning and maneuvering will have a much greater impact on how well your soldiers perform than any sort of rapid mouse clicking. The guns and various other weapons in Ghost Recon are instantly lethal. Not only is nearly every gun in the game capable of killing one of your soldiers in a single shot, most of them also have a very high rate of fire. This combination of high damage per shot and high rate of fire means that the most effective way to survive is to simply never give your enemy a chance to fire on your soldiers. In the world of Ghost Recon, stealth and surprise are your tools of survival.

 THE BASICS

This may come as a shock to gamers used to classic first-person shooters, but most soldiers are very inaccurate with any type of gun if they attempt to fire it while moving. This has been modeled into Ghost Recon, and if you're only familiar with less realistic first-person games, you'll quickly realize that the "run and gun" or "spray and pray" style of simultaneous rapid movement and rapid firing does not work well. Standard procedure in Ghost Recon is often as follows: a quick dash, a short pause accompanied by a volley of accurate fire, then a resumption of movement. Two minor exceptions to this rule however: If you are walking slowly in the standing stance, or using shuffle movement in any stance, you can take accurate shots while moving. However, in either of these cases, you still have to be moving slowly to pull off accurate shots. Not only does the foot speed of your soldier factor into how accurate your shots are, but the speed at which you are moving your aiming crosshair also affects your accuracy. If you attempt to make wild, fast movements with your mouse to quickly adjust your aim, you will notice your weapon pips will extend even farther away from the center of your crosshairs than if you were running.

As you can see from where the bullets are impacting into the ground, firing while running is grossly inaccurate.

Corners and stairwells are deathtraps in indoor combat. Approach these choke points very carefully; clear them out with some kind of explosive if you can.

Staying in one spot for too long can be dangerous, as it gives any enemies who have spotted you a chance to flank your position. When your soldiers are spotted and you need to make a retreat, use the run button and weave your soldier through any surrounding cover. If you are moving short distances, stay in the crouching stance. If you are going to tackle long distances, or simply wish to move faster, use the standing stance. It is often easier to use the crouching stance instead of the prone stance while attempting to line up a shot or scan the surrounding terrain. While the prone stance affords you a smaller silhouette, it makes you highly immobile and limits your field of vision. The standing stance does afford the advantage of letting your weapon pips re-center quickly after running, but otherwise it is more reliable to use the crouching stance. In any stance, try to line up your crosshairs on the enemy while moving, but hold your fire. This way, once you stop, you will not need to make any aiming adjustments that could possibly throw off your weapon pips. Simply line up the shot while moving, stop just long enough for the weapon pips to re-center a bit (about half a second), and then take 1–3 quick shots (or a small burst). Continuous auto-fire with anything other than a machine gun is a waste of ammunition, as each successive shot throws your weapon pips off even further. Sometimes it is more reliable to make small steps left or right to line up a shot rather than trying to track an enemy by following him left or right with the crosshairs.

As you can imagine, crouching or going prone reduces your outline and gives the enemy less surface area to target. However, what you may not realize is that the difference in eye level between crouching and standing stances is quite significant. When peering over a hill while standing, you may be able to fire upon an enemy you see at the bottom of the hill. Instead of merely retreating back over the crest of the hill when you begin to take return fire however, you can simply switch to a crouching or prone position and the enemy will be unable to see you. Playing a bit of pop-goes-the-weasel while on top of a hill, or near a building's window, can confuse your enemy as to your true location. Simply move near the window or hill crest, pop your head up, take a few shots, then disappear below the ridge line or window as you crouch back down. Be careful not to

Here, in the upright stance, you can see the enemy (and vice-versa).

Simply dropping to the crouching stance eliminates both your soldier's and the enemy's line of sight.

raise your head again in the same spot, however, as any enemy soldiers who may have spotted you will likely attempt to tag you in the head as you begin to stand.

A final note on movement is in order. It is easier to pick a moving enemy out of the terrain than an enemy who is stationary. However, it is also easier to quickly run up on a stationary target than a mobile one. While the single player campaign in Ghost Recon is oriented toward a slow, stealthy approach to your enemies, you will find there are more situations in multiplayer where you will need to quickly run up on a "camper" (a player who remains in one spot on the map for a long period of time). If the server is set to "arcade mode," speed tactics become even more important, as flanking a stationary enemy takes very little time.

The enemy soldiers here have chosen exceptionally poor places to stop and scan for targets. Be careful that you don't make the mistake of stopping in open terrain.

Two modern soldiers, each with roughly comparable skill and roughly comparable weapons, are placed on opposite ends of a forest and are ordered to kill the other. Which soldier will win? Most likely, it will be the soldier who spots his enemy first. For most practical purposes, this law holds true in Ghost Recon. If the enemy spots you before you spot them, the odds are good that you will be annihilated. In some respect, the mission structure of the single-player campaign gives you a noticeable advantage in this respect. Most of the missions are attack missions, meaning your soldiers will be moving in on an enemy that is not immediately expecting a firefight and may not be in the most feasible defensive positions. This fact gives you time; time to search and locate your enemies while not revealing your location to them. Once you have discovered your enemy's location, you can find the best angle of attack and commence the offensive.

There are several slightly different ways you can go about being stealthy. To highlight an extreme, you can put all your soldiers in the prone position and have them shuffle along the ground for the duration of the entire mission. This will offer a maximum amount of concealment and make it exceptionally difficult for your opponents to see you in most cases. However, this approach is tediously slow. While this tactic may be necessary in some cases, it is not necessary in the majority of cases. Effective ways to be stealthy vary

from map to map, because stealth is almost totally dependent on the environment. Sneaking across an open field in broad daylight is massively more dangerous than moving through a forest at night. As your troops make their way to their objectives, it is perfectly okay to take a break every few seconds or so and scan the area for effective terrain to conceal your advance. It would be nearly impossible to memorize the terrain of every map in the game perfectly, so you'll have to become adept at recognizing useful terrain on the move. Look for trees, bushes, buildings, rocks, and any other sort of impediment that will block a potential enemy's line-of-sight to your troops. Any sort of cover, even a small patch of over-grown grass, is better than no cover.

When you face off against a human opponent, you must change your tactics. While you should still try to keep your profile low and remain unseen, you must be aware that you no longer have the advantage of attacking an unsuspecting enemy. Human opponents know that you are out there and will be actively patrolling for your presence. Not only will they attempt to remain hidden while ferreting you out, they will also attempt to spot you from longer distances than a computer-controlled opponent might. Your human enemies will attempt to sneak up on you just as much as you are attempting to sneak up on them. To this

This soldier and his buddy behind him will never see the Sniper that takes them both out.

The terrain doesn't always provide for your troops. If you have to go over this hill, do it fast and get back into the underbrush.

extent, battles will usually be decided by which player is better at stealth and has a better understanding of the terrain. Knowing which locations on a battlefield offer the most cover with the broadest view of other locations is very important in multiplayer matches. With this in mind, it's probably a good idea to spend some time simply exploring the multiplayer maps and learning about the terrain and what kind of advantages different locations on the map offer.

Unfortunately for you, the terrain isn't always going to be friendly. Sometimes you're simply going to have to cross an open field in broad daylight to get to your objective. If there is a safer way around this field, take it, but sometimes you're simply out of luck. In a case like this, speed matters more than stealth. As a rough example, say you have three teams of two soldiers, all of whom must cross an open field. You should position four of your soldiers in spots that offer a good view of possible enemy locations, and then rush two of your soldiers across the field and into the nearest cover on the other side. Simultaneously rushing your entire team across an open field should only be used as an

emergency last resort or if you are absolutely sure there are no Snipers waiting for you to blow your cover before moving across. Leaving those four soldiers behind cover at least gives them a chance to out-snipe the enemy, should they attempt to cut off your soldiers crossing the field. Once your first two soldiers have crossed the field, position them in a spot to cover the rest of the soldiers as they cross the field in twos. If

Even with a stealth rating of 5 or 6, you won't make it past a Russian this close without being noticed.

THE THREAT INDICATOR

There is also another advantage that your soldiers have in the single-player campaign over their enemies: the Threat Indicator. It is quite possible that you will move within 40 m of an enemy's location and you will still not have discovered that an enemy is nearby. However, your Threat Indicator will light up at this point and inform you of a nearby foe. If you have a rough understanding of the terrain and where cover is available when your Threat Indicator lights up, you can slowly backtrack a bit and scan the area for enemies. You can use your Threat Indicator rather like a metal detector in this sense, slowly sweeping through areas and using it to hunt down enemies that may be out of sight. When playing against a human opponent, however, he will also have a Threat Indicator that will alert him to your presence. It is even possible for the server admin to simply turn off Threat Indicators altogether during multiplayer games. In either case, the Threat Indicator is only a specific advantage when facing off against computer-controlled opponents. Use this advantage to stalk your enemy and sneak up on him.

No Threat

No threats nearby... or so it seems

Threat Indicator

But shuffling forward a few steps reveals there is an enemy within 40 m.

your troops do get spotted while crossing the field, you have two plans of action. If you have no hope of making it to cover, or if you vastly outnumber the enemy, you can try to out-gun them and take them out by force before continuing your advance across the field. In a case like this, drop to the ground as fast as possible and lay down thick cover fire until you can line up some kill shots. If the gap between your soldiers and available cover is small, have them continue their dash across the field until they are safe, and then figure out the best way to stave off the enemy. As long as you pick a definitive course of action and don't panic, you should be able to save at least some of your team.

Stealth is important because it keeps your troops from being spotted and shot at. If your cover is blown, stealth immediately becomes useless and you should rely on speed instead. Get your troops out of harm's way in the fastest method possible and then worry about blending back into the surrounding terrain. Just how long you should keep running is a judgment call you'll have to make based on where your opponent is and how sure he is of your location. If you can get over a hill or other elevated terrain, you can prepare a quick ambush for any enemies that will follow. Quick changes between stealth and speed tactics can catch an unsuspecting foe off guard.

ATTACKING A POSITION

Since Ghost Recon is so dependent upon positioning and careful movement, there is a limited number of locations that provide both excellent cover and excellent views of possible enemy approach paths. If you know where these locations are, or can make a smart guess, you can use indirect fire or explosive weapons to clear them out before moving past them. Grenades (and in a pinch, maybe even anti-tank rockets) are designed for just this sort of attack. Rather than try to nail a spotted enemy with a grenade, attack a location or position where you suspect they may be. Don't go crazy with this tactic, however; explosions make a lot of noise. If you attempt to outguess your opponent and he's not at home, any enemies that might be nearby stand a good chance of being alerted to your position.

Odds are there are enemies hiding in this barn. A few M203 grenades will flush them out.

Be very careful when tanks are nearby, they have a very dangerous anti-infantry machine gun. Take it slow and careful around tanks.

SURPRISE ATTACKS

Once you've managed to detect an enemy without being spotted, you can formulate a plan of attack. If you are relatively sure of the safety of your position and are not in a rush, take a few seconds to watch your enemy and see how he behaves. Soldiers armed with sniper rifles make the best scouts because they can use the more advanced scopes on their rifles to scan for enemy movement from longer distances. Watch your opponent's movements, and position your troops in a spot that gives them a good view of where the enemy will be moving. You may need to switch your squads into Recon mode (so they withhold their fire) while they move into position or they may fire prematurely and ruin your surprise. Once your troops are in position, switch them over to Assault or Suppression mode and cut down your enemies.

If your opponent is not moving out in the open or is camping in a fortified defensive position, you're going to want to lure them out instead of engaging them on their home turf. At this point, you're going to need to create a distraction and draw the enemy's attention. Determine a point at which you are going to make an initial attack against an enemy that will draw their attention. Once you have figured out this initial attack position, select a few appropriate troops to make the attack. Snipers or troops with grenade launchers are probably your best bet for this job. Try to guess which venues of attack your enemy will use to ferret out your distraction and place your remaining troops in concealed locations to cover these attack venues. Once your cover troops are in position, move your decoys into position and commence the

A simple trap layout. Squad A gets the enemy's attention and draws them into the narrow pass ahead. Once trapped within the narrow pass, squads B and C can mow the opposition down.

distraction. Hopefully, the enemy will fall for the bait and move out of their defensive position to engage your decoys. If the enemy is limited or is not totally sure of where the decoy is attacking form, you can leave your decoys in position and continue to have them attack the enemy. If, however, the enemy is directly charging their position, your best bet is to retreat your decoy troops and pull the enemy farther and farther away from their defensive roost. As the enemy approaches your concealed troops, you switch them over to assault mode or suppression mode and have them cut down their foes from the side or from behind. The enemy at this point is caught in a pincher attack, with your decoy hitting them from one side and your cover troops hitting them from the other. In most cases, the enemy won't last for more than a few seconds.

After making some noise to the north with another fireteam the enemy quickly advances on their position, leaving them open to your cover troops who can quickly dispatch them.

As has been mentioned in this section, not all of these tactics are going to work against a human opponent. A surprise or decoy attack may not work exactly as planned against human opponents because they will be anticipating your

Two different scenes, one with night vision on, the other with it off. Night vision can help you pick enemies out of the terrain even in non-lowlight conditions.

STRATEGIES

cover troops to ambush them when they advance on your decoy. At this point, the battle becomes a game of who can guess where the ambush really is. If you suspect your opponent will attempt to outflank and counter-ambush your cover troops rather than rushing to attack your decoy, you can reposition your cover troops to cover the flanking routes. If your opponent is not attempting a counter-ambush, however, and instead simply continues to rush your original decoy, be prepared to have your decoys retreat very quickly. Technically, the number of ambush and counter-ambush setups you and your opponent can anticipate are unlimited, so just concentrate on the most plausible plans of action based on what the terrain allows. The

Before and after shots of a little Claymore Mine trap set by specialist Henry Ramirez for any guards trying to come down this tower.

more you know about your opponent's tactics, the location of his soldiers, and the immediate terrain, the better the odds are that you will be able to anticipate your opponent's strategy.

OUT OF SIGHT AND OUT OF HEARING

A combination of stealth, low light conditions, and a silenced weapon will result in the quick and unnoticed death of these two inept guards.

Not every weapon in Ghost Recon makes the same amount of noise or emits the same amount of light when fired. Firing a silenced pistol at an enemy from 5 steps away generates a lot less noticeable commotion than shooting them with a sniper rifle from the same distance. Large weapons, especially sniper rifles and machine guns, have bright muzzle flashes. The brighter the muzzle flash, the easier it is for an enemy to discover your location. Weapons with dim muzzle flashes or silencers are perfect for hitting an opponent from a concealed location without giving away your position. Even if your enemy outnumbers you, if they cannot pinpoint where you are, you can continue to attack them with impunity even after they are aware of the attack. As opposed to a massive simultaneous attack with many weapons, you can try a smaller attack with several quiet weapons and hope the enemy fails to locate your position before they are all dead. Soldiers with a high Stealth stat are perfect for this tactic. The most effective weapon in the game in this respect is the MP5-SD, a special silenced submachine gun that has a combination of range, firepower, and relative quietness that make it the ultimate assassin's weapon.

SUMMING IT UP

If you've read through this section and played a little bit of Ghost Recon, you should have a strong understanding of the game's strategic and tactical fundamentals. From here, you should have enough knowledge to begin to develop more specialized tactics and plans suited for the various combat situations in Ghost Recon. Remember to remain flexible and practice picking up on important terrain features on the fly. Similarly, remember that there are significant strategic differences in the way single and multiplayer games are played. You can use many tactics you develop in the single player game in multiplayer, but remember the differences in the gameplay between the two modes outlined in this chapter.

STRATEGIES

CHAPTER 5
Campaign Walkthroughs

MISSION I: IRON DRAGON

camp

location

PLATOON SETUP

Your choice of soldiers on this mission will be critical, not only because they are important for this mission, but also because they are important for future missions. You will want to begin to build up Command Points early, and refrain from losing anyone in order to maximize your Command Points.

Begin by selecting both of the Demolitions soldiers and placing them on either your B or C squads. Even if you decide not to use them for combat, you will want to have them earning Combat Points, because they will be vital for the completion of several of the upcoming missions.

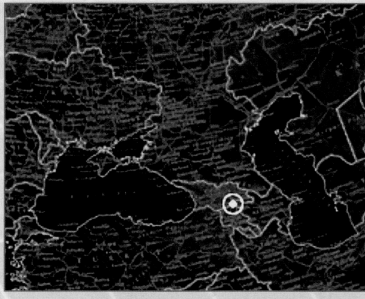

Next select a Sniper and place him either on the A squad or by himself on the B or C squad, depending on whether you prefer to have your Sniper grouped with others or alone. Once you have him selected, put at least one Rifleman or Support troop on squad A as well, and then fill in the rest of your team by selecting the most experienced Rifleman or Support troops, as fits your taste. Keep in mind that Riflemen are far more accurate, but Support troops can lay down some nice cover fire. When all of your troop types have been selected, you will need to select your equipment. Since this is the first campaign mission, choose varying kits for your soldiers so that you can see what you feel most comfortable using. You will not need to select any kit in particular for this mission.

South Ossetian Autonomous Region	
Sunny	April 16, 2008 05:45

OBJECTIVES

1. Neutralize Tent Camp Troops
2. Secure the Caves
3. Return to Insertion Zone
X - Capture Papashvili

MISSION I: IRON DRAGON

When this mission begins, you will find your troops in an open field. Fortunately there will not be any enemies around, so take a minute to check your troops and see how their weaponry reacts. The enemy should be far enough off that you will not draw their attention.

Once you're ready to move on, begin by setting all of your squads to Recon, then move them one by one to the west, along the rock wall that is slightly to the north of your position. When they are approximately halfway across the combat area, you should see two inclines to the west. Between these inclines is an enemy bunker, so be careful that you do not alert the enemy troops in this area to your presence until you have all of your troops in position.

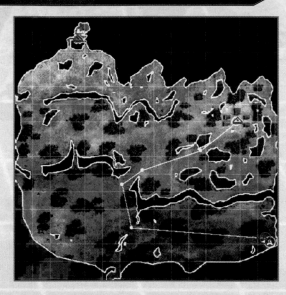

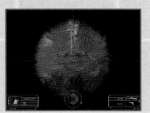

Your first kill.

Watch out! He's a good shot!

A cleared-out camp.

Switch to your Sniper when all of your troops have reached this position, and then order your squads to lay down suppressive fire at any enemy troops that approach your position. Use your Sniper to take out the soldier in the bunker. After you've taken him out, several more enemies should begin to approach your position, but your troops should be capable of putting them down relatively easily.

After the carnage ends, move your troops onto the eastern incline (the one closest to your current position), but do not proceed all the way up it. Switch to your Sniper and look to the north and you should see several ridges. On one of these is an enemy Sniper. Make sure that you take him out before going any further, or he'll lay your entire troop flat. Once he has been dealt with, proceed just east of his position and you will come to another incline, which heads to the north. If you prefer, you can simply charge into camp and take out the Russians at close range. Regardless of which method you use, head into the camp when you are done to make sure that you have dispatched them all.

From this position, atop the northern incline, have your troops head northwest by west and you will come upon the enemy camp. Providing your Sniper is still alive, you may wish to kick back at this point and slowly pick the Russians off one by one. If any of them approach your position then chances are the other soldiers in your squad will be able to take them out. On the other hand, if you prefer, you can simply charge into camp and take out the Russians at close range. Regardless of which method you use, simply head into the camp when you are done to make sure that you have dispatched them all.

○ SECURE THE CAVES & CAPTURE PAPASHVILI

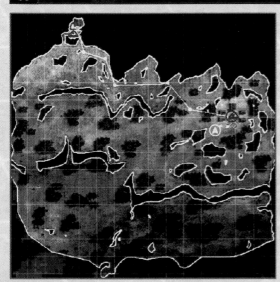

Once the tent camp troops have been neutralized, head north to the rock wall , and then head west along the wall until you come to the caves. Be sure to proceed with caution, as there are a couple of rebels standing guard outside of them. Take your time and kill any rebels that you see outside each of the openings to the caves. Once you have secured the outside of the caves, proceed inside.

Inside the caves you will have two or three more rebels to kill, but you will want to take only one squad inside, and make sure that the squad you do take in is set to Recon. Move slowly through the caves and take out any rebels that you see. Your goal here is to head to the far northern reach of the cave, where you will find a rather large cavern with Papashvili and one of his guards. Be careful who you shoot at here—you do not want to

accidentally kill Papashvili. Take out the guard, and then run up to Papashvili to capture him. Once you have captured him you will have completed all of your goals except returning to the Insertion Zone.

Papashvili in captivity.

Keep Low!

Remember to keep your troops low. Rarely, if ever, should you proceed while standing up— you become an easy target.

MISSION I: IRON DRAGON

MISSION I: IRON DRAGON

Be careful once you have captured Papashvili, as chances are you will find that rebel reinforcements will approach your position within the caves. Take them out, then head back to the rebel camp and begin to retrace your steps back to the Insertion Zone.

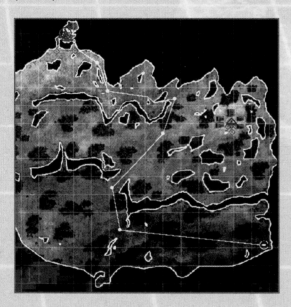

When you finally get close to the Insertion Zone, you will have one last firefight with several rebel troops. Take them out and then bring all of your forces to the Insertion Zone to complete the mission.

End of the firefight.

Alternate Route!

If you want a little more action on the way back to the Insertion Zone you can, instead of retracing your steps, head south from the caves. By doing this you will have to take your forces down two declines. At the second decline you will need to take out a rebel troop inside a bunker, but since he is expecting you to approach from the south, he should not be looking in your direction.

Once you take out the rebel troop in the bunker, proceed southeast down the next decline, then east toward the Insertion Zone to complete the mission. Keep in mind that you will still have that last firefight at the Insertion Zone to look forward to.

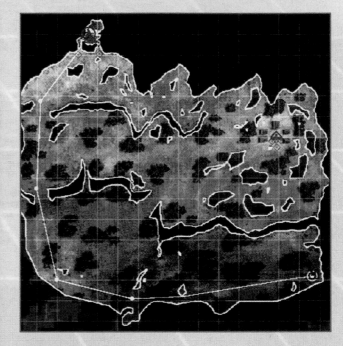

Take the rebel troop in the third bunker by surprise.

MISSION 1 IRON DRAGON

MISSION 2: EAGER SMOKE

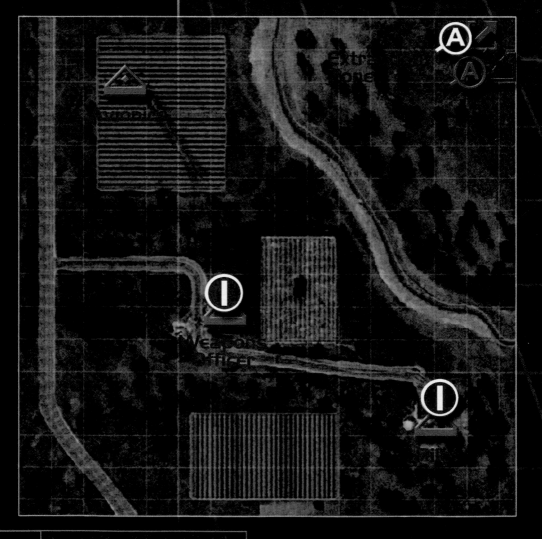

PLATOON SETUP

Now that you are more familiar with the different soldier types, you should have a better idea of what you prefer to use. In addition, you will have a specialist that you can bring with you if you choose, providing you were able to capture Papashvili on the last mission. Despite that, there are several troops that you will want to take for this mission. The first is at least one Demolitions soldier, but it is still better to bring both so that you can keep building up the Command Points on them. After that take a Sniper, as they are always extremely useful. Other than that you may fill in your platoon with Riflemen and Support soldiers as you see fit.

South Ossetian Autonomous Region

Cloudy

April 24, 2008
02:15

OBJECTIVES

1. Rescue Pilot
2. Rescue W. Officer
3. Get to Extraction Zone
4. Destroy Avionics

MISSION 2: EAGER SMOKE

MISSION 2: EAGER SMOKE

Because it is easy to accidentally clear out all of the enemies on this level before completing the optional objective, it is best to complete the optional objective first. To do this, begin by switching over to Night Vision and moving your platoon north to the fence. Next, head west along the fence until you cross a river, and then proceed with caution until you come to a field on your left.

When you reach the field, you will want to stop and lie down, looking out over it. Switch to your Sniper and zoom in, scanning the field. You should see quite a few enemies here, and you will need to take them out. Make sure that you

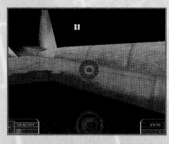

Laying the demo charge. It takes a while, so make sure all the Ossetian soldiers in the area are dead.

are lying prone to the ground, and begin to snipe them. They will slowly advance upon your position, but you should be able to snipe each one of them in time and, if not, then one of your other platoon members should prove quite capable of taking one or two out.

Proceed west by southwest into the field toward the downed plane. When you get close to it, switch to your Demolitions soldier and plant a demo charge on the plane to complete this objective.

You will have to take out quite a few Ossetian fighters here.

Alternate Route!

If, for one reason or another, you would prefer to skip destroying the avionics, then you will be able to take a more direct route to the Weapon Officer's position.

Simply head southwest and, after some time, you will reach the position. Keep in mind, however, that if you take this route then chances are you will encounter several Ossetian troops on their way to the Weapon Officer's position, and in addition, several of the Ossetian troops that are guarding the avionics will converge on your position anyway. As a result you will often find yourself fighting more enemies than you had planned, and it will end up being just as easy to take out the avionics to begin with, though you will save yourself the effort of taking out a few Ossetian troops that you may not have had to.

RESCUE WEAPONS OFFICER

From here head south by southeast toward the next objective and continue until you see a house. Once the house is in sight you will want to approach with caution, as there are Snipers inside. Instead of approaching head on, approach from the west and take out the guards outside of the house. When the guards have been dealt with, go in close and walk around to the north side of the house. You will find an open window; shoot any Ossetian soldiers that you are able to see through the window, and then go to the south side of the house and enter through the back door.

Once inside the house, secure the lower floor and walk up the stairs. Immediately to the south you should see the Weapons Officer. Kill the Ossetian that is guarding him and check the other room on this floor for a Sniper. Once both have been dealt with, walk up to the weapons officer before heading out of the house.

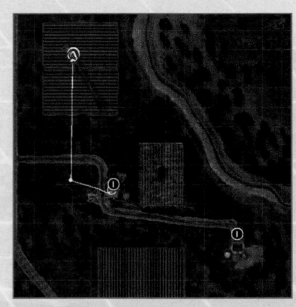

Be careful, you will find several Ossetian soldiers in there!

(Above) The Weapons Officer after being freed.

RESCUE PILOT

that are inside. While doing this, however, be extremely careful not to hit the pilot, as he is in the center of the barn on the ground floor.

Once you have taken out as many of the Ossetian troops as you can see, begin to approach with

Captors killed, the pilot is able to stand up freely now.

caution. When you are close enough to see up to the second floor, take out the Sniper on the second floor on the south side of the barn and continue to take out any

To rescue the Pilot you will next need to head south across the road, then turn and head west toward the barn where you will find the pilot. Be careful once you get

close, as you will have to deal with several guards, and a couple of them can be well hidden if you are playing on the harder difficulty levels.

After you have taken out the troops that are outside the barn, you will want to maneuver around to the north side of the barn, all the while keeping a distance. Once you reach the north side of the barn, look toward the barn and you will be able to shoot the Ossetians

other Ossetian troops that are inside. After all of the Ossetian troops around and inside the barn have been taken out, the pilot will stand up. Use this as your signal to proceed the rest of the way in to rescue him.

GET TO EXTRACTION ZONE

Now that you have rescued both the pilot and the weapons officer you will need to head back to the Extraction Zone. To get there, have your troops head north and cross the river. After you cross the river begin to proceed slower as there are several Ossetian troops in the trees on the other side of the bank. If you wish to take them out, head a little northwest by north until you see them. If you wish to avoid them, simply head north until you reach the extraction zone.

MISSION 3:
STONE BELL

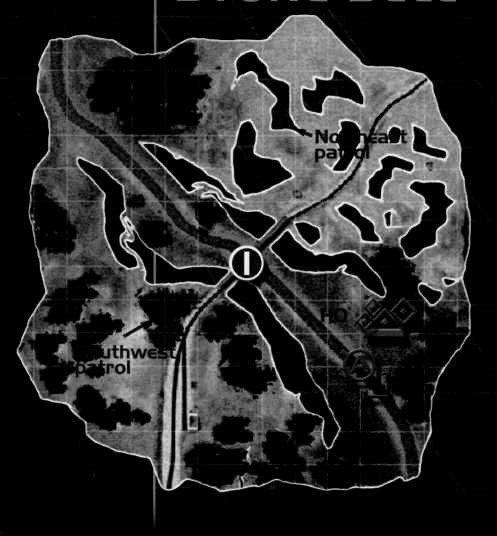

Northeast
patrol

Southwest
patrol

HQ

PLATOON SETUP

To begin, make sure that you select both of your Demolitions soldiers, as you will need to take out two tanks on this level—if one of them misses too many times, or dies, the other will be paramount. You will want to place them in their own squad, as they will need to stay near where you start the mission.

Next select a Sniper and place him in his own squad. You will need to have the Sniper watch over the bridge on this level while the rest of your soldiers take out the enemies that come up the incline and cross the bridge. The Sniper should be able to provide excellent cover, especially considering the distance.

OBJECTIVES

- 1. Destroy Northeast Patrol
- 2. Destroy Southwest Patrol
- 3. Prevent HQ Breach
- x - No NATO Casualties

South Ossetian Autonomous Region

Sunny

May 2, 2008
10:00

Other than that, you may fill in your primary squad with whatever troops you wish. At this point I suggest taking both of the Specialists, as they should have more allocated Command Points than any of your other troops, and their weaponry is more useful. If you do not have any Specialists, or only have one, don't worry; your ordinary soldiers will be quite capable of handling the job at this point.

The only other consideration you have at this point is what kits to choose. For the most part they do not matter; however, you will want both your Demolitions officers to be packing an M136 so that you can take out the tanks that will approach you on this level.

Do not worry overly much about silenced weaponry, however, as you will find yourself in one rather large firefight, and almost all of the Russian troops will hear you.

DESTROY NORTHEAST PATROL

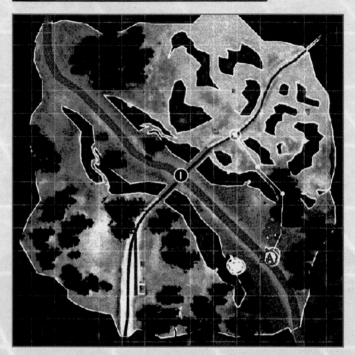

Begin by moving your Demolitions troops into the bushes along the wall of the cliff to the west of your starting position, a few feet away, and leave them there. You will need to switch to them quickly if you hear tanks, so just keep them in mind.

Take the rest of your platoon and move them northeast behind the Georgian house into the trees. Head northwest up the incline and toward the railroad tracks.

When you get to the railroad tracks, stop there and kill Russians until you complete the first objective: Destroy the Northeast Patrol. You will have to be careful, as you are rather exposed, but you should only have to kill approximately four before you will complete the objective.

Stay here to take out the Northeast Patrol; they will come over this ridge and you can take them out at your leisure.

MISSION 3: STONE BELL

DESTROY SOUTHWEST PATROL

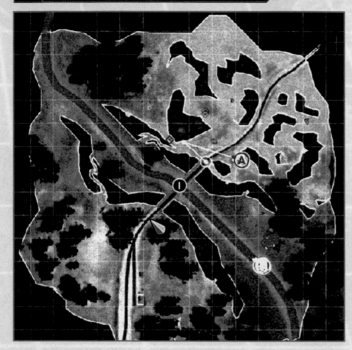

Leave your Sniper here to slowly take out the Southwest patrol.

Next move your squad along the railroad tracks to the southwest until you reach the bridge. Once you arrive here, listen for the tanks, and if you hear them moving, switch to your Demolitions officers and have them move toward the bridge until they can see the tanks; then have them blow up the tanks.

As for the rest of your squadron, you will want to entrench yourselves and kill Russians as they come toward you. Have your Sniper, if you brought one along, lie down on the railroad tracks and watch the other side of the bridge. You should see one or two Russians walking around on the other side and, when you do, snipe them.

Eventually a group of Russians will make an attempt on your position and will begin to move up an incline that is slightly to the west of the bridge on this side of the ravine. Continue to take them out and slowly move toward it until you are standing at the brink. Once you

reach this position, take out everyone that you can see before returning back up to the bridge.

The way across the bridge should now be clear. Begin to move your squad across it carefully. Chances are, there are still several Russians from the Southwest Patrol on the other side. Upon reaching that side, carefully hunt them down until you have completed this objective. Because they move around, there is no definite place that they will be; however, there tend to be one or two slightly to the north of the tracks.

PREVENT HQ BREACH

At this point you've taken out most of the threats, and all you need to do is mop up whatever remains of the opposition. To do this, begin by moving your forces west along the ridge on the south side of the ravine. When you come to a decline that will let you into the ravine do not go down it; instead continue along the ravine, looking over it every now and then, and take out any Russian troops that you find. If the mission does not end before you reach the bottom, continue along the road, killing any Russian troops that you see.

Once all the Russian troops have been eliminated the mission will end. Providing that you do not let any Russians past your position while completing this objective you will also complete the optional goal and no Georgians will have died.

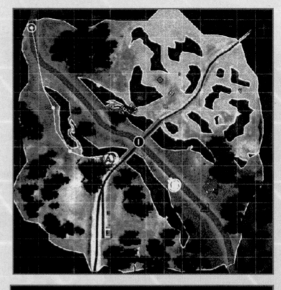

The last of the Russians— take them out to end the mission.

Try the North Side!

If you have problems on the south side of the ravine and find yourself getting shot up then do not be afraid to head along the north side of the ravine. Sometimes, due to the way that the Russians have positioned themselves, you will find that side to be easier. Normally, however, you will have to encounter more Russians at close range on that side.

MISSION 3: STONE BELL

MISSION 4: BLACK NEEDLE

Troops

Crossro

PLATOON SETUP

Even though your new specialist is a demolitions officer, he is unable to use demolitions charges. Despite that, the extra anti-tank weaponry will be a big help later on.

OBJECTIVES

1. Secure the Crossroads

2. Contact UN Troops

3. Return to Extraction Zone

X - Keep UN soldiers alive

On this mission you will not have a need for any type of soldier in particular. You may find a Sniper handy for taking down a few of the enemy, and you will likely want to bring your Demolitions troops with you in order to keep building Command Points on them, but it is not necessary. You may have noticed, providing you were able to keep from having any Georgian casualties on the last mission, that you have a new Specialist, and a Demolitions soldier at that. Despite this, if you look through his kits you should see that he does not have any demolition charges, which means that your ordinary Demolitions soldiers will still prove very important on the later levels.

The one thing that you will want to do while setting up your platoon is try to divide your forces into two squads. You may wish your Sniper to be in his own squad, and that's fine just so long as you plan which squad to put him in later on. Lastly, there is no particular importance to the kits that you choose on this mission, so simply choose whatever you feel most comfortable with.

SECURE THE CROSSROADS

After the Russians in the first booth have been taken care of, carefully cross the bridge and take out the two Russians near the booth on the other side. Once they have been dealt with you will need to move your forces slowly toward the town that is to the northwest of the second booth.

Proceed with caution, as you will find quite a few Russians guarding the town here and you will need to take each and every one of them out in order to secure the crossroads.

Begin by having your troops head west by southwest until you see a bridge. When the bridge is in view, begin to approach with caution, as there are a couple of Russian guards in the booth before the bridge. Make sure that you take them both out quickly as, if you take too much time, one of them will run to the booth on the other side of the bridge and alert the guard there.

The first guard booth. Make sure you take out both of the guards near it.

CONTACT UN TROOPS

Once the crossroads has been secured you will want to split your platoon in two and have squad B head into the wooded area to the southeast of town. Here they will lie in wait to prevent anyone from flanking you while you have squad A head to the north to engage the Russians that have the UN soldiers pinned down.

After heading to the north for a little ways you will come to a large rock formation. Head to the north side of the rock formation before turning and heading north by northeast. Continue this way until you have gone just over halfway across the map to the east, and then turn south and you should see what looks like several ruined structures. You will need to be excruciatingly careful in this area, because not only are you very close to where the UN soldiers are pinned down, but you will also have to deal with one or two Russian patrols here. Once the Russian patrols have been dealt with, turn toward the ruined structures and approach with caution. This area is swarming with Russians, and you will need to take each of them out before they take you out.

To do this from a relatively safe distance and position, proceed around the eastern edge of the complex and then around toward the street. When you are able to round the corner of one of the buildings and stare down the street, get low and have your Sniper take each of the enemies out one by one. This way the Russians have to deal not only with you but also with the UN troops, and as a result they will not approach you as fast as they may otherwise.

Unfortunately the trek to the Extraction Zone is not easy. After contacting the UN troops, the Russian reinforcements will arrive, and they will advance on you from the crossroads. It is for this reason that squad B was left behind.

After contacting the UN soldiers, order squad A to head toward the crossroads and switch to squad B in order to prepare for a firefight. If you have positioned your forces well this should not be overly difficult. You should be able to take several of the Russian reinforcements out before squad A arrives. When they do, make sure that you are careful with them. They can provide quite a bit of assistance but you will want to keep them out of harm's way in order to keep the UN soldiers alive.

After the Russians at the crossroads have been dealt with, chances are you will have eliminated all resistance. If you have not, however, continue to move your troops across the bridge and back to where you started. When you get back to where you started the mission will end.

Upon cresting this hill, squad A will have to enter the firefight.

After you cross back over this bridge you will enter the home stretch.

MISSION 5: GOLD MOUNTAIN

OBJECTIVES

1. Secure the bank

2. Investigate Crash Site

3. Go to Extraction Zone

X - Avoid Civilian Casualties

On this mission you will not only have to take out Russian Snipers but you will also have a Russian tank to deal with. As a result you will want to make sure that you bring your own Sniper and that you are packing an M136 to take out the tank in case you get stuck.

Fortunately, providing you have been able to keep up with the Specialists so far, you will have a new Sniper to use this time around, and his L96AI should prove far more useful than your other Snipers' M24s. While your specialist Demolitions soldier will be able to handle the tank threat on this mission, you will still want to bring along both of your other non-Specialist Demolitions soldiers in order to continue building the Command Points on them. Other than that, fill in your squadron however you see fit.

The only kit that you will want to make sure you have on you is a kit that includes an M136 for the tanks, as stated above. Other than that, choose whatever kits you feel most comfortable with. You will be going into a building, however, so you will want to make sure you are carrying some weaponry with silencers.

Avoid the Snipers!

On this mission, as on other missions, make sure that you watch out for Snipers. Not only does this mission have the two Snipers to deal with in front of the bank, but there is also one overlooking the crash site from the west.

The hidden Sniper - watch out for him when you investigate the crash site!

Tbilisi, Republic of Georgia

Sunny

May 14, 2008
09:00

SECURE THE BANK

When the mission begins you will want to head north to the crossroads and then turn west. Proceed west until you have to turn to the north again, then continue forward toward the steps. Walk up the steps so that the bushes will be between you and any enemies to the east.

The area behind the bank should be free of enemies until you open the door.

Continue along toward the north until you have to go down the steps ahead of you, then turn east and sneak to the north side of the building that should be in front of you, near the white vans parked there. This is the rear entry into the bank and should enable you to storm the bank without putting yourself in as risky a situation as a frontal assault would.

Don't approach the front of the bank; the Snipers with the fixed machine guns on the upper floor can rip your party to shreds.

Open the door in back, but make sure that you are standing to the right of it. Slowly creep around and take out the Russian that is guarding the back room here. After he has been shot continue to open the door on the far side of the room and proceed slowly into the main area of the bank. In here you will have to take out several Russian soldiers. Do not move too far out into the bank, as there are two more upstairs and they will shoot you from above if you give them the chance. After you have taken out the Russians on the ground

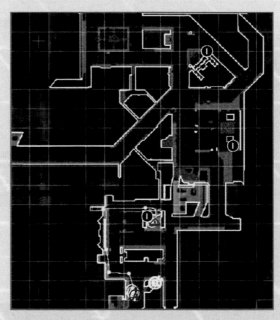

floor of the bank, move toward the stairs to the west, but before you climb them turn up and to the east to take out one of the Russians above. Once he falls dead continue up the stairs to the landing.

Now that you have are halfway up the stairs, proceed with caution up the second half. At the top of the stairs you will find another Russian. Kill him, then proceed around to the far side of the room and you will see two doors. In each is a Russian manning a fixed machine gun. Take them out and you will have secured the bank.

The lower floor of the bank—quite a few bodies laying around down there.

The first alleyway. This should be right behind the bank.

After the bank has been secured, leave through the back again and head through the alley to the north. Be careful at this point. You will end up passing refuges from time to time as you go through this area and you will want to make sure not to shoot them lest you fail the optional goal on this mission.

If you choose to make life easier for yourself later on, kill a few of the Russians out here now.

When you come to a T in the alley, stop. If you want to make things easier on yourself later you may head down the right side and take out a few of the Russians there, but afterward head back to the T again. When you are ready to resume your journey, head west down the left branch of the alley and you will emerge facing a street on the west side of the map.

The second alley— remember to take the further one!

Continue north and slightly to the northwest and you will see two alleyways that head to the northeast. Take the second one that you come to, the further one, and head along it keeping to the north until you emerge on another street.

At this point you should be near the crash site. Proceed slowly forward and take out each Russian that you see. There will be several here, so expect a firefight. After they have all been dealt with proceed toward the downed chopper to complete the second objective.

Finally the crash site— make sure you take out the Russians guarding it before getting too close.

GO TO EXTRACTION ZONE

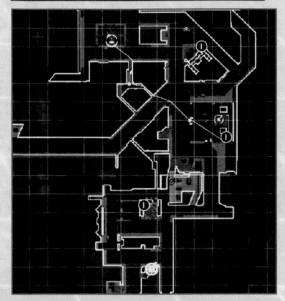

Take out the Russians within the compound before you attempt to head for the roof.

Since you have just inspected the crash site, you will need to be on your guard. Almost immediately a tank will come at you from the southeast and several Russian troops will approach you from the west. If you are quick enough you can choose to flee back down the alley that you came from; otherwise you can stay and fight. Because your position at the crash site is rather heavily fortified, with walls to hide behind, you should not have an overly difficult time dispatching those troops who make an attempt on your position.

Once you are ready, head back down the alleyway that you came from and this time head west when you get to the T. After you emerge into the street you will

probably need to take down a few Russians, if you did not earlier. With the Russians cleared out of the way, proceed northeast toward the walled compound here and duck down, then enter through the front gate, killing every Russian that you see inside.

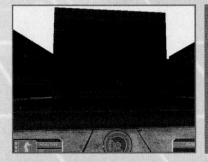

As if the tank weren't enough, you will have troops coming at you from either side of this building as well.

After the Russians on the ground have been taken out look up and you should see two on the roof. Use your Sniper to bring the two of them down, then proceed to the south side of the building inside the compound and you will see a flight of stairs. Simply run up the stairs and bring your squadron to bear on the helipad and the mission will end.

At long last the tank; take him out fast as he'll give you problems later on.

Just ascend these and you will be on your way to freedom!

MISSION 6: WITCH FIRE

PLATOON SETUP

This mission takes place in the dark, and Night Vision will enable you to pick enemies off at a distance. Your Sniper is going to be very important on this level. Using your specialist Sniper would be ideal; he is capable of taking out a group of guys at a distance because of his increased ammo capacity. You will also need to take out a mobile SAM launcher, and your specialist Demolitions officer should come in handy as well. Not only will you be able to take out the mobile SAM launcher, but many of the Russians are clustered together and are quite easy to take out from a distance with a rocket.

OBJECTIVES

1. Gather Intel from SE House

2. Gather Intel from NW House

3. Get to Extraction Zone

X - Destroy SAM Site

Other than those two soldiers, it is still always a good idea to bring the two initial Demolitions officers with you to continue to build command points on them, and a support soldier may be helpful because he will be able to lay down a rather large amount of suppressive fire. In the dark when you can't quite see where your enemies are at times, this can prove extremely beneficial. Once you have chosen your key troops, simply fill in your party as you see fit, and select any kits that you feel comfortable with, provided you remember to bring the M136 to take out the SAM launcher.

Izborsk, Russia

Clear (night)

June 6, 2008
02:00

MISSION 6: WITCH FIRE

Begin by heading north by northeast from your current position until you come to a road. Once you reach the road crouch down and proceed slowly, and you will eventually come within sight of the mobile SAM launcher.

Upon reaching this location, set your team for Recon so that they do not fire before you are ready. After

you ready your forces, begin to move toward the SAM launcher until you are in range before ordering your squadron to lay down suppressive fire and attempting to take out all of the Russians who are guarding the site. You will need to do this fast because not only are there quite a few Russians guarding the SAM site, but several of them are manning fixed machine guns as well. After they have been dealt with, move in with your rocket launcher and take out the mobile SAM launcher.

After crossing the road, make sure you keep your head down; the Russians are close.

The SAM site. Be careful here, as you will have quite a few Russians to deal with—and some are manning fixed machine guns.

Alternate Route!

If you are having problems taking the SAM site, you can choose to skip it if you wish. Instead of heading for it in the beginning, start by heading east by northeast and you will come to the Southwest House. Remember that if you do this you will not circumvent the Russians guarding the Southwest House. It is also important to note that you will not get another specialist after this mission if you choose to skip the SAM site.

One blown SAM, one completed objective.

MISSION 6: WITCH FIRE

GATHER INTEL FROM SE HOUSE

Once the mobile SAM has been taken out, head to the south up over the ridge, then turn and head east by southeast toward the SE house. Use extreme caution as you approach the Southeast House, however, because you will have quite a few Russians to deal with as you near it, and many more may end up flanking your position from a collapsed area in the castle wall to the northwest of it.

Fire a few volleys at the soldiers outside the house, then proceed in. After you have taken out the Russians outside the house, continue slowly forward and shoot any enemies that you see coming out of the house. Chances are a few will pour out through the door on the side.

While you are shooting the Russians that are coming out of the house, chances are you will come under fire from the northwest. When this happens, turn around and shoot any baddies that you see coming at you from the collapsed area in the castle wall. Unfortunately, however, they do not all come at once, so you will have to wait awhile and snipe them as they come, but while you are doing this make sure that you prevent any Russians from coming out the side of the house and putting you in the crossfire.

Here you can see several Russians grouping around a fire— pick them off fast, because more will come out around you.

Quite a few Russians will come at you from the northwest, but that also means you will get quite a few kills taking them down!

After you have finished dispatching the Russians that are preventing you from entering the Southeast House, simply head in and inspect the site to complete this objective.

Don't get too close to the ruined wall yet or Russians will pour out of it.

Quite a few bodies on the southern side...

These Russians should fall easier than the previous ones; there aren't as many of them.

In the first bedroom there is not one but two Russians to deal with. Make sure you don't forget the second.

Now that you've gathered the first bit of intelligence, head out of the Southeast House and move east until you are able to turn northeast along the castle wall. Continue in that direction until you come to the collapsed portion of the wall.

Here you should see several Russians around a fire. Take them out with a silenced weapon, if you are able, then continue north by northeast. The first house that you will come across will house several Russians and, while you do not need to take them out, you may wish to anyway to ensure that you do not have to tangle with them later.

Move fast within the closer house; some of them are hard to hit without getting hit yourself.

If you decide to take out the Russians in the first house, head through the front door and shoot each in turn. There should be approximately three of them and they will all be within view, so act fast. After they have been dispatched head to the second house to the northeast.

There are also three Russians in this house and you will need to take them out. Enter slowly and take all of them out and, after you have canvassed the house, you should end up completing this objective.

The second house. Complete the second objective in here.

MISSION 6: WITCH FIRE

⬡ GET TO EXTRACTION ZONE

The last Russians you will have to deal with before completing this mission.

From this point head northeast toward the opening in the wall and you will be on the road heading north. All you need to do is continue heading north from here and you will come to a raft; the Extraction Zone. On the way, however, will be another contingent of Russian soldiers. There should be quite a few of them, so take them out carefully.

Get as close as you can to the raft with all of your troops to complete the mission.

Through this wall is the extraction zone, and the Russian guards

After you have taken them out continue north toward the raft. The mission will end when you get close enough to the raft.

If you make too much noise gathering intel from the NW house the soldiers that would normally be near the Extraction Zone will come up and ambush you while you are still in the NW house.

MISSION 6: WITCH FIRE

MISSION 7: PAPER ANGEL

West Pylon

East Pylon

PLATOON SETUP

For this mission you will need to have both demolitions charges and some anti-tank weaponry in case you need to take on the tanks that are guarding the bridge. As a result you will want to bring both of the Demolitions soldiers that you started with and have them carry demolitions charges in case one gets taken out. In addition to that, have your specialist Demolitions officer bring an M136 so you can tango with the tanks.

You may also want to bring a Sniper so you can take out a lot of the Russians on the far side of the river without even needing to get within range of them. Fill in your platoon as you see fit. Other than the kit assignments mentioned above, you can also use any kit that you like for your troops.

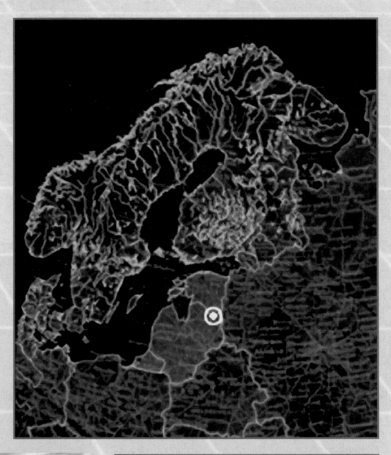

MISSION 7: PAPER ANGEL

OBJECTIVES

1. Destroy East Pylon

2. Destroy West Pylon

3. Get to Extraction Zone

X - Eliminate Camp Garrison

Lubana River, Latvia

Sunny

June 10, 2008
06:00

DESTROY EAST PYLON

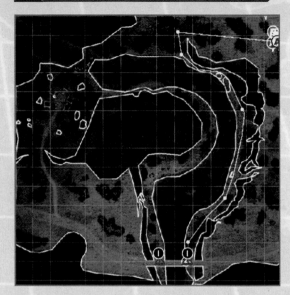

look across the river and take out the two on the far side. Once the Russians guarding this area have been taken out proceed to plant a demolition charge on the east pylon.

Your first kills on Paper Angel.

Several Russians in the distance; be careful, as more tend to be on the west bank.

The Russians from the west bank. You can wait for later or take them out now, but it is easier to deal with them while they are on the opposite side of the river from you.

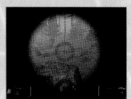

Begin by heading west by southwest along the rock ledge until you reach the end of it. From here turn south and you should come to the river. Upon reaching the river, proceed with caution as there should be a Russian patrol near here. If there is take them out; if not you will have to take them out soon.

Continue heading south by southeast along the river until you come to another squad of Russian soldiers. Take them out but then look across the river and you should see two more squads. Switch over to your Sniper and take them out while you are able to, then continue along the river.

After a short time you will eventually come to the bridge. It is absolutely imperative that you keep quiet here and use silenced weaponry as, if you make too much noise, then you will bring quite a few Russian troops down on you from above.

Your Threat indicator will go red in this area, but ignore it; it's useless here since it is not only indicating the enemies on your plane, but also those on the one above you. Instead, proceed toward the bridge and take out the guard that is next to the pylon, then

Looking across the river. Make sure you take out the two Russians over there so you don't have to deal with them when you are on that side.

MISSION 7: PAPER ANGEL

ELIMINATE CAMP GARRISON

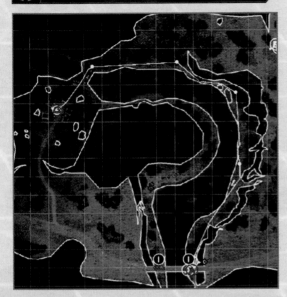

The Russian camp. If possible take them all out from this distance so that you don't run as high of a risk of getting shot.

Now that you have planted demolition charges on the eastern pylon, proceed back along the river to the north and, when possible, northwest. Eventually you will come to a crossing point.

Upon reaching the crossing point, hide out in the bushes and begin to snipe the Russian soldiers that are within your sight. Be careful. The Russian soldiers in the camp will attempt to cross near you and take you out, so if you are using your Sniper, make sure to have the rest of your squad lay down suppressive fire. After all the soldiers have been dispatched, walk toward the camp and make sure that all the Russians near it are dead.

The cleared out camp; once they've all been terminated it is so peaceful here...

MISSION 7: PAPER ANGEL

DESTROY WEST PYLON

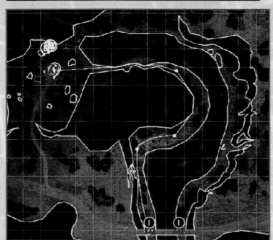

From the Russian camp head directly east and you should come to what appears to be a small canyon. Head through the canyon and follow along as it continues to bend toward the south. Provided you were able to kill the two squads of Russian troops earlier that were on the western side of the bank, the trip should be rather uneventful until you are in sight of the western pylon.

On the western side of the river the Russian troops on the plane above you have a far easier time of seeing you. As a result you will need to proceed slowly and with caution after issuing recon orders to your soldiers. If you are careful and quiet enough then it is possible to get to the pylon and plant a demolition charge on it without getting spotted.

On the other hand, if you do get spotted, act quickly and decisively. Watch the place where they are able to walk from above the ridge down to the riverbed to the north of the bridge because they will come down to your level in large numbers. After you have either snuck past the enemies or killed them, proceed to the west pylon and plant your demolition charge.

Here is the canyon; make sure that you don't miss it and go the long way, as this will be much safer.

More Russians that you hopefully killed while on the other bank. Since they've already dead you won't need to make any noise killing them now.

Keep quiet and close to the water; don't let these guys know you're here.

The Russians that you killed earlier; they will pose no threat now.

Objective completed, time to bug out!

GET TO EXTRACTION ZONE

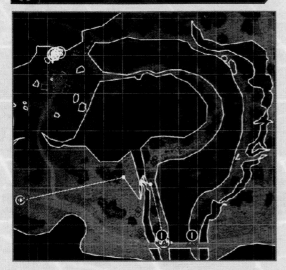

Now that both pylons have been destroyed and you have managed to eliminate the camp garrison you will need to head to the Extraction Zone. To do this head north along the river until you come to the area that you can use to reach the top of the ledge. Walk up to higher ground, then turn around and head north by northwest toward the trees. After you reach the trees, turn back west by southwest and proceed toward the Extraction Zone until you crest a hill.

Upon cresting a hill, you should see a crossroads that is guarded by quite a few Russian troops.

The way up, just make sure that you immediately head north once you are up to prevent getting spotted by the Russian tanks

Organize your troops in such a way that you will be able to take out the Russians guarding the crossroads, then open fire. After you have destroyed the Russian patrol, proceed to the extraction point and complete the mission.

The reason that you want to have your forces head north by northwest immediately is because if you head directly toward the

extraction zone you risk running into several Russian tanks that were guarding the bridge. If you wish, you may take them out, however there is little reason to do this.

Here are the tanks on the close side of the bridge and on the far side of the bridge. Make sure you stay away or they will kill you.

Make sure that you get them all rather quickly; if you let even one of them live for too long, you may end up being the one who is lying on the ground dead

MISSION 7: PAPER ANGEL

MISSION 8: ZEBRA STRAW

PLATOON SETUP

whom you feel most comfortable with, then select whatever kits you want, making sure that anyone who can carry anti-tank weaponry does so.

OBJECTIVES

1. Secure the Village

2. Destroy East Artillery

3. Destroy North Artillery

X - Protect Friendly Tank

Your new specialist on this mission will be a Demolitions officer, but since you do not need any demolition charges on this mission you may not wish to bring him. Instead, expect to take out a couple of tanks; you will want to again bring your two original Demolitions soldiers along and possibly the first Demolitions specialist. In addition to that, make sure that you have a Sniper. You will have quite a bit of mist here and he will be able to take out Russian soldiers at a distance far more easily than the rest of your soldiers.

You may also want to bring one or two soldiers whose primary weapon has a silencer on it, but that is not a necessity. Simply fill in your platoon with the soldiers

MISSION 8: ZEBRA STRAW

Venta, Lithuania	
Rain	June 24, 2008 16:00

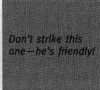

The moment this mission begins, take positions within the rubble near you and order your entire platoon to lay down suppressive fire. Within about ten seconds you will find your position overrun by Russian troops. If you are careful, however, you will be able to escape this altercation unscathed.

The ruins of an old building. Hide here fast so you don't get slaughtered within the first minute.

After the firefight is over, proceed north by northwest from the rubble through a ruined part of the wall, then continue to the northwest. You will shortly come upon a tank that is almost immediately blown up. After watching it erupt into fire, continue to the northwest

One Russian tank, blown to bits.

until you approach what looks to be a church. Take out the Russians that are near the church, then continue to walk through the rubble here and take out any Russians on this side of the street. Run to the other side of the street and take out each Russian you see there. After all of the Russians have been taken out, you will have secured the village.

Don't strike this one—he's friendly!

It is important that you make sure that you shoot at Russians and not friendly forces. Behind the friendly tank coming up the road from the west are several friendly soldiers, and you do not want to shoot your own men. Check the map from time to time to see where they are so that you know when you may be aiming at one of them.

Here there are three Russians outside an old church. Kill them before they take out your tank.

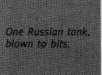

You will find Russians hiding in both of these buildings; don't let them get you before you get them.

DESTROY NORTH ARTILLERY

Next, head north from the village until you are within sight of the artillery. It should not be far, but you will have to take out several Russians along the way. Once you are within sight of the northern artillery, fire an anti-tank rocket at it to destroy it.

Be careful running through here; sometimes on your way back you will come across another Russian or two.

The northern artillery; blow it and complete the objective.

DESTROY EAST ARTILLERY

Finally, head east by southeast and you will come to the east artillery. There may be a few Russians around it, and if there are, kill them. For the most part, however, it should be unguarded. Fire a rocket at the east artillery and the mission will end.

Take out the Russians on the hill before you get to the east artillery or they will double back on you.

The eastern artillery: blow this one and you will not only complete the objective but also finish the mission.

MISSION 8: ZEBRA STRAW

MISSION 9: BLUE STORM

PLATOON SETUP

For this mission you will be able to take whatever soldiers you want. You will be fighting in the rain on an overcast day, so visibility will be limited at close range. Despite that, the Sniper is still able to pick people off at a distance, so he may prove valuable. In addition you may still want to bring along the two Demolitions soldiers simply to keep building Command Points on them.

As for kits, bring any kit you want. The only thing to keep in mind is that you will probably want silenced weaponry to take the first island so you don't make too much noise and alert the Russian officer. Other than that, it really doesn't matter too much; this will be a search and destroy mission.

One thing to keep in mind at this point, however: you may want to define a team of six people now that you have most of your options open to you, and try to stick with them, arranging them in whatever order you prefer for each mission. This helps in building Command Points to maximize your team's potential. The more you switch around between officers, the worse off you will be in the long run.

OBJECTIVES

- 1. Clear Northern Island
- 2. Clear Eastern Island
- 3. Clear Western Island
- X - Capture Russian Officer

 Nereta Swamp, Latvia

Rain

July 3, 2008
09:00

Begin by heading north, past the dilapidated structure near your starting point, and continue until you are within sight of the eastern island. Do not approach too quickly, as there is a bunker with a Russian Sniper. Instead, approach slowly and take him out as soon as you can with your own Sniper.

The Russian bunker; approach with care. There are more than one in there.

The Russian officer; you will need to run up to him while standing, and do it fast, in order to capture him

Your Sniper's gun should alert the rest of the Russians on the island, and they will come charging toward you. Take them out as they come, and don't be a slouch, as there are quite a few on the island.

Beware the Bunker!

Be careful at the southeastern end of the northern island. There is a Russian bunker hidden by the trees. Take out the Russians there before they can regroup and hide.

After you have eradicated the Russian resistance on the eastern island, continue inland and search their camp—not only the close section but also the section to the northeast near the pole. Then head into the shallows toward the northern island to the northwest. Along the route you should see another Russian soldier. Now, because you have already cleared the east island, you should know not to shoot at this one: this is the Russian Officer.

Unlike the first mission, where you captured Papashvili when your Threat Indicator was not red, your Threat Indicator will be red near the Russian Officer on this mission. The reason is simple: if you don't get to him fast enough, or if you alert him, he will pull out a gun and you will have to kill him. On the other hand, if you run straight at him before he can draw his weapon then you will be able to capture him.

They will be coming at you from both sides, so keep alert. Otherwise it may be you lying face down turning the water red.

Remember, don't leave this island as soon as it says you have cleared it; make sure you capture the Russian officer first.

MISSION 9: BLUE STORM

CLEAR NORTHERN ISLAND

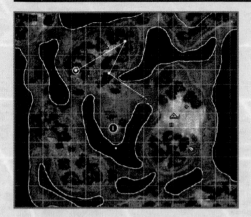

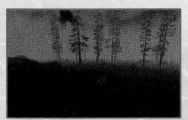

A line of
Russian
casualties
after clearing
the beachhead
of the
northern
island.

*They don't
even know
what is
coming.*

Now that you have captured the Russian Officer, you will need to head to the northwest toward the northern island. Fortunately there are far fewer Russians on the northern island than there were on the eastern island, but you will have to hunt them down.

To do this, proceed north to the northeastern end of the northern island. From there turn and head to the southwest, patrolling back and forth along the island until you have taken out all of the Russian soldiers on it. After they have all been killed you will complete this objective.

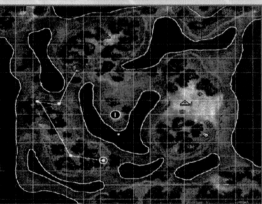

 ## CLEAR WESTERN ISLAND

To clear the western island, begin by heading west by southwest until you reach the island. On the northwestern tip of the island you will come to a Russian camp. Make sure you approach with care and take out the Russians guarding the swampy recesses to the north of it before heading in to take out the camp.

Now that the patrol has been dealt with, circle the Russian camp, taking out anyone that you can see or who comes near. After they have been dealt with proceed to the southeastern tip of the western island and kill any Russians you see, until they are all dead and you complete the objective, and thereby the mission.

*The Russian
camp on the
western
island. You
will find
Russian troops
scattered
about it.*

*Another
mission done,
another
specialist
earned.*

MISSION 9: BLUE STORM

MISSION 10: FEVER CLAW

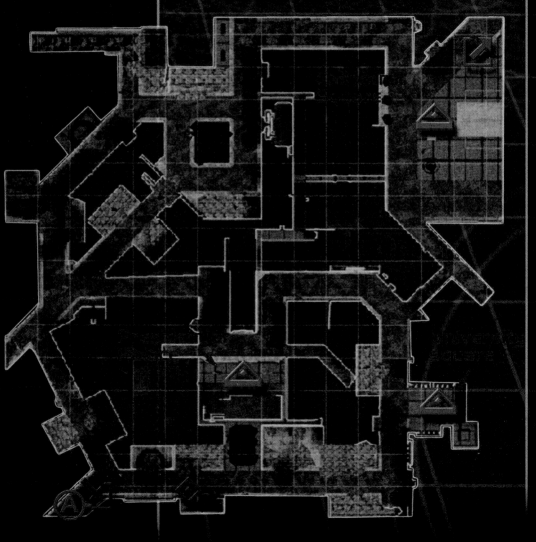

PLATOON SETUP

This mission is by far the trickiest mission yet in the game. Your goal will be to escort several friendly tanks, and if you want to get the next specialist, you cannot let any one of them be destroyed. To compound this problem you will need to move quickly, as they will not wait for you.

As a result you will, most likely, need to use only one squad on this mission. Of course, it is still good to bring as many backup soldiers along as possible, if for no other reason than to amass command points on them. However, chances are you will not have time for them.

The thing that makes this mission even trickier, and dictates your choice of soldiers, is that you will run across nine Russian tanks during this mission. There are two ways to take them out: Either follow your tanks and let them blast the Russian tanks at each turn, leaving you to take out the enemy soldiers before they launch a rocket at your tanks, or run ahead of your tanks and take everything out ahead of time.

Because the easiest way to keep your tanks alive on this mission is to rush ahead of your tanks, the best choice of soldiers for your primary squad are your two Demolitions soldiers you started out with, along with the specialist Demolitions soldier you received several missions ago. By selecting the M136 as secondary weapon for all of them, you will be able to take down nine tanks on this mission, providing you don't miss. The thing that makes this difficult is the fact that you will need every one of those rockets.

OBJECTIVES

- 1. Secure University Square
- 2. Secure Presidential Palace
- 3. Secure Cathedral Square
- X - No friendly tank casualties

Vilnius, Lithuania	
Rain	September 1, 2008 18:00

This is the safest place from which to launch rockets at the two tanks guarding University Square.

The two tanks guarding University Square. Nail them quickly before they are able to shoot at you.

Proceed with caution, Russians tend to come out at you from both sides of the street.

Begin by running up the street alongside the tanks on the northern side of the road. Continue running until you come to a lump of rubble with a demolished car next to it, then slow down and proceed forward with care. Take out any Russian troops you see, and when you come to the corner of a building on the northern side of you, be extremely careful: There is a Russian tank on the other side of the building.

Move forward and switch to your anti-tank weaponry, then take out the tank while keeping outside of its firing arc. After you have destroyed it, switch back to your main gun and take out any Russian soldiers near it before they can fire upon your tanks. After they have been dealt with continue to run ahead of your tanks and cross to the southern side of the road.

The first tank: Take it out fast, along with its entourage.

Continue running forward along the southern side of the road until you come to more rubble. From here proceed slowly forward and take out any Russians that

you can see. Order your squad to lay down suppressive fire as well to ensure that the Russian opposition is taken down quickly. After you take them out, turn to the northeast and you should see two Russian tanks. Fire a rocket at each of these to destroy them. You will have to do this at a rather long distance, however: if you get any closer they will take a bead on you and shoot you.

After you have taken out the two tanks, proceed toward them shooting any Russians that you see and, before your tanks actually arrive, you should be able to take out any that would pose a threat. Once they have been killed you will complete your first objective.

SECURE PRESIDENTIAL PALACE

Now that you have secured University Square, your tanks may take a few moments to arrive, then they will regroup before trudging ahead. Use this opportunity to put some distance between them and yourself by continuing forward to the north. Be careful here, as chances are you will need to take out a couple of Russians on the eastern side of the street. After that proceed to the northwest.

Shortly the street will bend around to the west. Continue along, but make sure you are zoomed in with your weapons. There is a patrol of Russians that guards this area, and you will need to take them out before continuing farther. After they have been dealt with, keep west even when the street bends to the south until you can see a tank to the south.

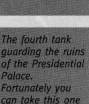

Watch out when running down the street here, as a Russian patrol tends to be at the far end.

The fourth tank guarding the ruins of the Presidential Palace. Fortunately you can take this one out at a long distance.

With the fifth tank you will need to be more careful; get the rocket ready and fire right after you step out from behind the truck.

Use a rocket to blow this tank, then head south along the eastern side of a street behind a wrecked truck. From behind the truck, slowly head south until you can see another tank to the west. Quickly switch to your M136 and fire another rocket to take this one out. Be careful while doing all of this. There are several Russians in the Presidential Palace and you will need to take them out to make this area safe.

After taking out the Russians within the palace you will be ready to move on to Cathedral Square.

If, after destroying the second tank, it does not indicate that you have secured the Presidential Palace, then head south up the rubble ramp to the second floor of the building there. From this point proceed through the corridors and see if there any Russians inside of the building. If there are take them out; if not head out and search the area and take out anyone you see.

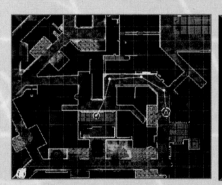

Squad Management!

If you want to make use of your secondary or tertiary squads, upon reaching the crossroads after securing the Presidential Palace you may wish to order them to the crossroads, then finally to the square that is to the northeast of the crossroads. This helps because then you will have another squad in the square, where quite a few of the Russians lay in wait, ready to take out your tanks.

MISSION 10: FEVER CLAW

Once it indicates that you have secured the Presidential Palace, head north via the western route and then turn west when the road does. Continue until you near the massive crossroads and crouch down and look around. You should see two to three Russian troops in the area.

Take the Russians out, and if you are still well ahead of your tanks, have your soldiers run to the northeast really quickly and stop under the arch. From here take out any Russian troops that you see, then head back southwest. The reason this can help you is that it gets rid of some of the Russians you would have to face later on.

Now that you are ready, go north from the crossroads and continue as the path bends to the northeast, then finally east. At this point you should arrive at an area where the road makes a square pattern with a lot of grass in the center.

Patrol around this road and take out any Russians that you see. Unfortunately there are deceptively more in this area than may be apparent at first. Make sure that

The Crossroads presents several opportunities— your tanks will head north from here.

you enter the theater along the eastern side, because there is at least one Russian there. After you have secured the area proceed north, then east.

This small park holds a rather deceptively large group of Russians, and they tend to be well hidden. Make sure that you patrol it well

It can be easy to miss the Russian inside the theater unless you know to look for him there.

Take out the sixth tank while you can barely see it, then continue east, taking out each of the other three front tanks when you can just barely see them.

When you reach the end of the next street turn and you should see three tanks near you. Take them out quickly along with the Russian troops that are near them. After it is relatively secure, proceed slightly to the south and you should see a fourth tank. If you haven't missed any of the tanks use your last rocket to take it out, or wait for your tanks to do the job. In the interim simply make sure that you take out any Russian soldiers. After everything here has been destroyed the mission should end.

Finally the ninth tank. Once it is destroyed, and all the Russians here have been killed, the mission will end.

MISSION 10: FEVER CLAW

MISSION II:
DREAM KNIFE

PLATOON SETUP

MISSION 11: DREAM KNIFE

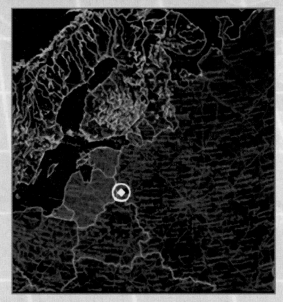

OBJECTIVES

1. Secure an entrance

2. Rescue NATO POW's

3. Go to Extraction Zone

X - Rescue Moroshkin

	Ljady, Russia	
☾	Clear (night)	September 16, 2008 03:00

This mission takes place at night, within a Russian camp. You will want silenced weapons on anyone that can carry them, and the two specialists with silenced weaponry really shine here. Even though you may also want to bring along a Sniper, it is best if you do not bring them with your main squad. While it is quite an asset to take along someone who can hit a soldier at a distance, the shot will also most likely set off the alarm, and you want to avoid that. Instead, it is best to place him on squad B or C if you do bring him along, in order to build Command Points.

Other than that you will not face any significant threats, so simply fill in the rest of your platoon with whomever you want to build Command Points on. Keep in mind, however, that on the next mission you will need more demolition charges than any one of your Demolitions officers can carry. As a result it is recommended that you continue to build Command Points on your two initial Demolitions officers.

○ SECURE AN ENTRANCE

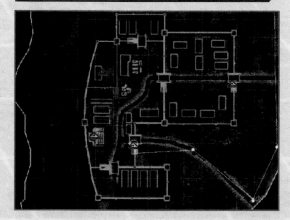

Begin by issuing Recon orders to your squadron, then switch to Night Vision. After you are set up, move south along the fence. After a short while you will come to a command post. Kill the Russian in here, then look to the west. You should see Entrance 1.

Use a silenced weapon to take out the Russian standing guard in the guard post so you don't alert the Russians who are guarding Entrance 1.

If you like, take out the two guards outside of it and the one in the tower next to it. This will secure an entrance, and complete the objective, but it is better to continue to entrance 2 instead, since that is closer to your objectives. In addition there are two Russians that patrol and will come to entrance 1 soon, so take them out before they see the dead bodies and set off the alarm.

Continue to the south and you should come to another guard post. Kill the guard in here as well, then begin to head northwest along the road that is near the guard post. Down the road a little way you will come to Entrance 2. Take out the two guards that are standing outside, followed by the guard inside the tower to secure this entrance.

The patrol will come around the corner and spot the downed guards near Entrance 1 if you don't take them out as well.

Quickly take out the two guards who are standing guard outside, as well as the guard in the tower; otherwise they will signal the alarm and the compound will be crawling with Russians.

RESCUE MOROSHKIN

MISSION II: DREAM KNIFE

Walk across the courtyard toward the medical building, then enter through the front. From here head toward the first door and open it, shoot the Russian in here, then proceed toward his body and open the door next to him. Slowly peek your head through the door and snipe the guard that is on the southern side of the room.

Continue out into the room, toward the opening on the west side of the room and shoot the Russian in here, then go into this room. Here you will find Moroshkin; walk up to him and he will follow you.

In order to proceed into the camp you will need to take out the Russians that are guarding the gate next to Entrance 2.

Next, head through the door that is slightly to the south of the gate that the guards were guarding. Walk up the stairs here then continue to the other side of the room and down the stairs on the other side. Be careful, however, as you open the door. Once it is open you should have several Russians to take out, so kill them, then step out the door.

Moroshkin is hiding in the medical building, guarded by three Russians.

Camping Spot!

If by some chance you do accidentally set off the alarm, the hospital is one of the best places to camp out. Simply lay down in the entrance to it and snipe the Russians as they pass by. You should be relatively shielded from enemy fire until the whole thing blows over.

If you happen to set off the alarm, you should be able to hide in the hospital and take out the Russians that come for you in relative safety.

Here is one of the three guards who is guarding Moroshkin.

After taking out the third guard, run up to Moroshkin to get him to follow you

RESCUE NATO POWS

From the hospital head north, then turn west and run along its northern wall, then head north again. By the time you reach the wire that surrounds the POWs you should have made it behind where the Russians are holding the POWs. Shoot at the Russians that are guarding them to remove the resistance, then walk through the door in the fence and up to the POWs.

After taking out their two guards, the POWs will join you on your way out if you run up to them.

Snipe the Search Lights!

If you are having problems with the exterior search lights, simply take one of your silenced weapons and shoot them out. It may take several shots, but afterward you will be able to proceed in relative darkness.

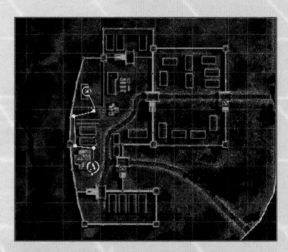

EXTRACTION ZONE

To reach the Extraction Zone, head back to Entrance 2 and exit there. Then head south and continue until you reach the edge of the camp. Turn west and run until you can head north again. Continue north and you will come to a Russian patrol. Kill the Russians and proceed to the Extraction Zone to end the mission.

(Left) On your way around the prisoner camp you will need to pass by one last Russian patrol.

MISSION 12: IVORY HORN

PLATOON SETUP

OBJECTIVES

- 1. Plant Demo in Sub Pen 51
- 2. Plant Demo in Sub Pen 52
- 3. Get to Extraction Zone
- X - Plant Demo in Fuel Depot

For this mission you will need to be able to plant three Demolition charges. As a result you will need either the Demolitions specialist who has demolition charges and one of your initial Demolitions soldiers, or both of your initial Demolitions soldiers. Chances are you will also want to have one or two soldiers whose primary weapon has a silencer. Fortunately, this will be the last mission that you will need more than one Demolitions expert for.

Fill in your party with whomever you wish. While a Sniper is of some assistance, you will want to keep quiet on this mission to prevent the alarm from going off. The only kits that are of any particular importance on this mission are the Demolitions charges; otherwise select whatever you are most comfortable with.

Murmansk, Russia

Clear (night)   September 22, 02:00

MISSION 12: IVORY HORN

MISSION 12: IVORY HORN

Begin by setting all of your forces for Recon and switching to Night Vision, then head up the ramp, turn east, and walk toward the large barge. Once you are against the barge, turn south and follow along its length, taking out any Russians that may spot you.

After a short distance you will come to a crane. Walk just past the crane and turn west, continuing along and you will see a large cement ledge. Move along the north side of this ledge, being careful to not stray too far out or Russians inside the warehouses on the south side of the ledge may spot you.

Upon reaching the end of the ledge you should see a decline that you can walk down onto the sub within Sub Pen S1. Walk down onto the submarine and plant your first demolition charge here to complete this objective.

Turn south upon reaching the barge, but watch out for the Russians south of it.

Go just past the crane before turning to the west.

The planks here can make more noise than you may feel comfortable with, and they may alert the Russians.

By placing your demolition charge on the submarine, you will complete this objective.

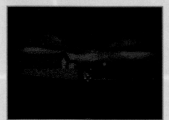

Keep close to the ledge as you run below it; otherwise you may end up spotted by Russians.

Keep Quiet!

The lower you are to the ground the less chance there is of being spotted or heard. As a result, duck or crawl along the planks if you wish to pass a guard without killing him. Keep in mind, however, that any other soldiers who are grouped with you will affect the amount of noise that you make as well.

PLANT DEMOLITION CHARGE IN FUEL DEPOT

From the sub, proceed south up the incline and continue toward the large cement wall. Upon reaching the wall turn east and go to the edge of the stone wall. From here look to the south, ensure that no guards are passing by, and run across the open area to the east, hiding against the north side of the next stone wall.

Continue along this wall until you find an incline to the south, then walk up the incline and go east toward the center of the Fuel Depot. Upon reaching the Fuel Depot, plant a demolition charge and you will complete this objective.

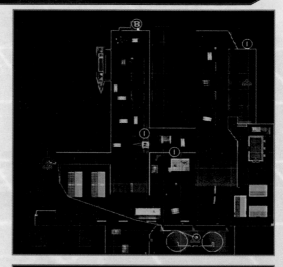

Make sure that there are no Russians, then run across this expanse and you should safely make It to the other side.

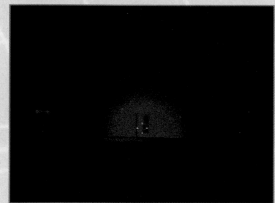

Plant the demolition charge near the center of the two storage tankers to complete this objective.

MISSION 12: IVORY HORN

PLANT DEMOLITION CHARGE IN SUB PEN 52

Head north down the decline here, then turn east and proceed until you near a building. At the building turn north and continue until you reach the Sub Pen. Walk north along the sub pen until you come to the second opening on its western side. Enter here and you will emerge on the lower level of the Sub Pen. Kill the Russian patrols inside of the Sub Pen. Walk the length of it when you think that you have killed them all to make sure your Threat Indicator does not turn red.

After you are sure that it is safe, walk along the plank to the submarine and plant your third demolition charge on the sub.

Head south from the Fuel Depot in order to reach Sub Pen S2.

The third demolition charge; after this you will need to head to the Extraction Zone.

GET TO EXTRACTION ZONE

Exit the Sub Pen and head to the west, toward the area where the barge is docked, then head south until you are able to turn to the west again. Turn west when you are able and continue until can turn north. From this point head north cautiously.

Between you and the Extraction Zone should be a Russian patrol. Unfortunately they are fairly accurate, so you will have to spot them first and take them out fast. Once they have been dealt with, continue to where you started the mission, which is the Extraction Zone, and the mission will end.

The Extraction Zone is on the other side of the barge.

The Russians will ambush you on your way back to the Extraction Zone, so be careful.

MISSION 13: ARCTIC SUN

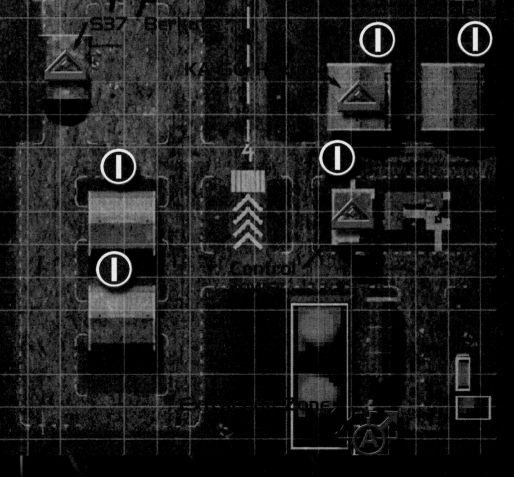

MISSION 13: ARCTIC SUN

OBJECTIVES

1. Secure Control Tower
2. Destroy S37 Berkut
3. Destroy KA-50 Hokum
X - Get to Extraction Zone

Arkhangel'sk, Russia

Cloudy   October 3, 2008
                                   04:00

For this mission you will need to bring along a Demolitions officer to blow the enemy aircraft, as well as a Sniper. Early on you will be infiltrating a tower, and when you are at the top of the tower you will have an opportunity to take out several Russian patrols without even putting yourself in the line of fire.

Other than that you will have no special need for any particular soldier type. Since you are now able to use all of the specialists, you should know your options well, so choose the troops with whom you are most comfortable. The only kit you will need to take is the one that contains demolition charges for your Demolitions officer; the other kits may be chosen capriciously or by reason, whichever you prefer.

SECURE THE CONTROL TOWER

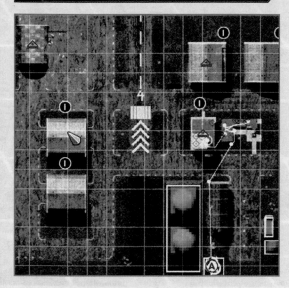

clearing them out. The only thing to be aware of is that because of the close proximity, the moment one of them yells or a shot is fired, the rest will likely converge on your position, so be prepared for an intense fight.

After the compound has been cleared proceed into the actual control tower. Now that the reserve garrison has been dealt with it will be far easier to take the control tower. Enter through one of the doors on the eastern side, and as you did in the compound, go room to room taking out Russians. Once the first floor has been cleared, climb the stairs and take out the Russians in the upper control room.

Begin by switching over to Night Vision and proceeding toward the north, along the paved stretch. In a short time you will see a large tower stretching three stories into the air. Next to this is what appears to be a small compound.

Go to the eastern side of the compound and enter through the door there. Inside you will find quite a few Russians, and you will need to go room to room

Make sure you search all the rooms in the compound; there is a surprising number of Russians here.

Get the Russian on the far side of the tower when you reach the top, but be careful. You will have to get very close to him first.

In order to secure the control tower, you will need to secure not only the tower, but also the compound next to it.

MISSION 13: ARCTIC SUN

DESTROY KA-5O HOKUM

MISSION 13: ARCTIC SUN

With the control tower cleared out, you may wish to take a few minutes and, if you have a Sniper with you, or even Tunney with his SA8o, look out the upper windows. From here you will be able to see much of the mission area and can take out quite a few Russians without even having to get within firing range. Once you are done, proceed down and out the northern door of the control tower.

From the northern door of the control tower, head north to the hanger containing the KA-5O Hokum, then along to the western side. Open the door on this side and go in, then open the next door. In the hanger you will need to take out the Russian guard, and then plant your demolition charge to complete this objective.

The door on the west side of the hanger takes you to a chamber from which you emerge into the hanger. Be careful when opening the second door, though.

If you want to take out a few Russians before facing them on the ground, this is a golden opportunity.

If you have approached the hanger silently, then the Russians guarding the KA-5O Hokum won't even hear you coming.

DESTROY S37 BERKUT

In order to destroy the S37 Berkut, you will need to leave the hanger of the KA-50 Hokum the way you came in and head west. You will need to walk for quite a ways but eventually you will come to a rather small hanger. Take out the Russians guarding the exterior and continue inside.

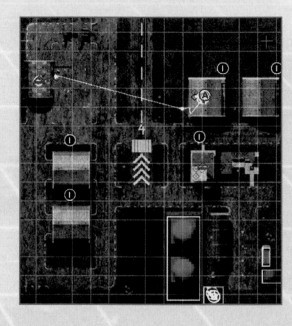

Near the S37 Berkut is a fixed machine gunner; don't round the corner into the hanger too fast or he'll get you.

Inside you will find a Russian manning a fixed machine gun. Take him out and plant a demolitions charge under the S37 Berkut.

GET TO EXTRACTION ZONE

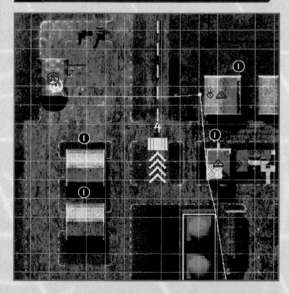

From the hanger that was housing the S37 Berkut, head back east to the hanger that was housing the KA-50 Hokum, then south toward where you began the mission to reach the Extraction Zone. Upon arriving, the mission will end.

Upon crossing the gate, you will arrive back at the Extraction Zone and the mission will end.

MISSION 13: ARCTIC SUN

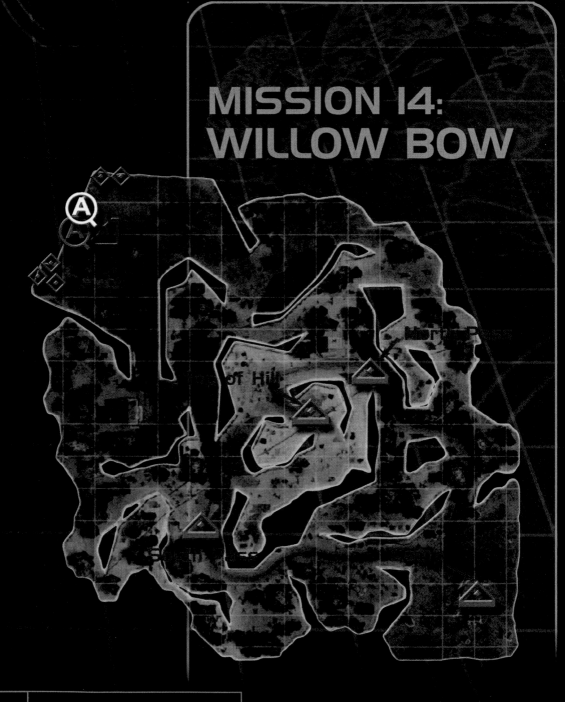

MISSION 14: WILLOW BOW

PLATOON SETUP

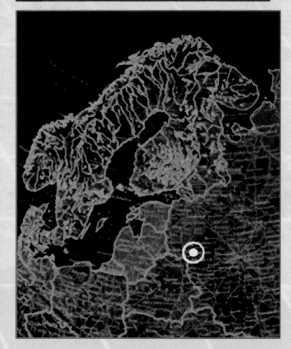

OBJECTIVES

1. Take North Pass

2. Take South Pass

3. Take Top of the Hill

X - Neutralize Russian Camp

While you will not need a Demolitions officer for this mission, you will need one for the next, so it is important that you continue to bring along at least one soldier capable of wielding anti-tank weaponry. Other than that, the one soldier who is still especially helpful is your Sniper, whoever that may be. He is not strictly necessary, but because you will be crossing rugged terrain where you may find yourself in the sights of a distant enemy, you may find that the Sniper is quite useful on this mission.

There is no one kit that is particularly important. At times it can be difficult finding some of the Russians, so you may wish to bring sensors, however, some of the other kits can be just as helpful.

Toropec, Russia

Snow   October 23, 2008
13:00

MISSION 14: WILLOW BOW

TAKE NORTH PASS

Begin by heading east until you reach a cliff face, and then follow along it as it turns to the southeast. Somewhere along here you should hear gunshots and your Threat Indicator should turn red. When this happens, look up and take out the Russian that is watching from above. After he has been taken out, continue along the cliff face to the southeast.

Head up the first incline that you come to, turn to the east and approach the corner of the cliff face slowly. You will need to take out two patrols near the cabin that is beyond that cliff face, so cautiously walk forward and kill any Russians that you see.

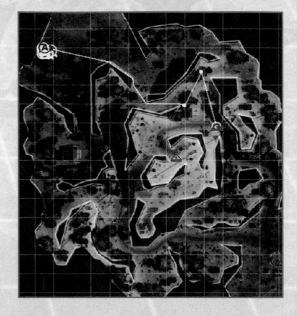

Watch out for this Sniper; if you don't get him now he will pick off your patrol as you pass by.

By taking them out one by one as they come around the corner, you will end up taking out an entire patrol or two here.

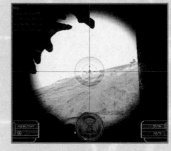

After rounding the corner, make sure that you immediately take out the two Snipers to the south; otherwise they will not only shoot at you but also lob grenades.

While you are attempting to take the north pass, a friendly tank will come up the ridge and secure the area. Do not mistake it for a Russian tank.

It is important that you watch out above during this firefight. At the top of the hill there are two Russians who are acting as Snipers and can hit you from a distance, as well as lob grenades at you. You will need to take at least one of them out or you'll be under constant fire in this area.

TAKE SOUTH PASS AND TOP OF THE HILL

Search the area where the incline is, then after a quick search continue to the northeast and you should come to the last of the Russians in this area. Take out the Russians that are near the top of the hill, then if you have completed the second and third objective continue onto the next, otherwise proceed to the area where you still need to complete an objective and search it more thoroughly until you have completed the first three objectives.

Unlike the soldiers guarding the northern pass, the Russians that guard the southern pass tend to intermingle with the soldiers that guard the top of the hill. As a result, chances are you will have to visit both areas before completing either objective.

To do this, head due west along the cliff face from which the Russians were firing, near the top of the hill. Continue until you come to an incline to the southeast, then kill the Russian that is northeast of there, and finally continue to the southwest, skipping the incline.

After a short distance you will come to a large rock that offers some cover. Kneel down here and check out the area. There are two Russian bunkers with fixed machine guns in them, as well as a Russian patrol nearby.

Take out all of the Russians you can see, then patrol the south pass to make sure that you have not missed any. When you feel that you have taken out every Russian in the area, proceed northeast of the position marked as the south pass on your map and proceed up the incline that heads to the east.

Even though the rock on the right may offer cover, if you aren't careful the Russians will advance on your position and you will need to take them out.

Make sure that you get the Russians in each of the bunkers; if you forget one of them then the Russians in the other bunker who have not forgotten you will get you

After taking out the Russians in the bunkers, walk toward the southern bunker and you will find several Russians on the far side of a rock formation.

Since you have already taken out the Snipers when securing the northern pass, there should not be many Russians on the hill for you to mess with.

MISSION 14: WILLOW BOW

NEUTRALIZE RUSSIAN CAMP

From the top of the hill proceed southeast down the decline, then turn north toward the north pass. You may run into a few Russians near the north pass; if you do, then take them out.

From the north pass turn southeast along the mucky dirt road and continue as it winds its way west, then south toward the Russian camp. Head a little way to the south, but do not go far. Instead keep some distance, and from this vantage point you should be able to snipe the Russians that are holding the camp. Continue to pick them off one by one and after a little bit you will complete the objective.

Passing by the north pass again on the way to the camp.

If at all possible, avoid actually entering the camp because with the amount of firepower that the Russians have it will be a very difficult firefight.

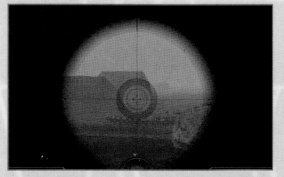

Simply snipe each of the Russians in the camp. After they have all been dealt with, the mission will end.

MISSION 15: WHITE RAZOR

Spasskeya Tower

MISSION 15: WHITE RAZOR

On this mission two types of troops are going to prove paramount: a good Sniper and a Demolitions officer with anti-tank rockets. If you still have Tunney, the specialist Demolitions officer, then you should definitely bring him along, as he will give you an extra shot in case you miss one of the tanks or decide to use the anti-tank weaponry against a pack of Russian soldiers. If you do not have him, or if you prefer not to use him, a regular Demolitions officer should suffice.

The first half of this level will play out like most any other mission; however, after you have secured Nikoiskaya Tower, you will have to cross a long courtyard with Russians and Russian tanks. As a result you will often come to long expanses with enemies at the end. By using your Sniper you will be able to take them out without getting dangerously close.

Other than the Sniper and a Demolitions officer or two, you will probably want to bring along a support soldier. His machine gun will prove invaluable, simply because once you enter the courtyard where Nikoiskaya Tower is, you will need to mow down quite a few Russians. Besides these soldiers, however, you may simply fill in your platoon as you see fit. The only kits that are important are the Anti-Tank Rockets on the Demolitions officers.

OBJECTIVES

1. Relieve pinned down troops
2. Take Nikoiskaya Tower
3. Take Spasskaya Tower
X - Avoid Civilian Casualties

Moscow, Russia

Snow

November 10, 2008
11:00

RELIEVE PINNED DOWN TROOPS

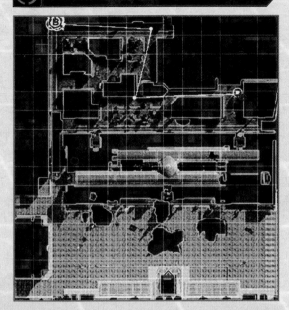

On rounding the corner, make sure you take out the first Russian patrol that you see.

Make sure that you take out the Russians that you can see during your approach.

While you may take your time for the rest of the objectives on this mission, you must hurry through this objective—otherwise the pinned-down US troops will be killed. In order to rescue them in time, you need to order your squad to lay down suppressive fire and run to the east until you cannot head east any further. From here turn south and head through the park along the street and between the two buildings up ahead.

If you shoot one of your guns too early, you may find yourself facing off with the Russians in the park before you want to. If you do then make sure to use the wall in the park for cover.

At this point you should run into the first of two Russian patrols. Take out the first, then head east a little bit to take out the second. Once they have been dealt with, turn back east and run down the street.

While heading down the street, zoom in with your primary weapon and you should see one or two Russians. Take out whoever you see, then continue until you can turn south again near the pinned-down US troops. On turning south you should see several more Russians.

Assist the US troops in the firefight here. You should have approximately two Russian patrols to deal with. Once you have killed them all you will have completed your objective, and the US troops will head back the way you came.

Once you round the corner, take out the rest of the Russians that are harassing the US troops and you will complete this objective.

◯ TAKE NIKOISKAYA TOWER

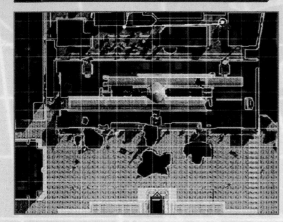

From the point where you freed the US troops, head south into the building near them. Continuing into the building you will shortly come to an open area where there is a patrol of Russian soldiers. Take them out, then look up, and somewhere along the upper catwalk you will see another patrol of Russian soldiers. You will need to take them out as well to proceed; if they are not there yet, wait for them and take them out as soon as you can see them.

Go west until you come to an opening to the south. Walk into the opening and up the stairs, then head back north to the catwalk and resume heading west on the second floor.

Proceed until you can no longer head west, turn north along the footbridge, then turn and head west until you can head south across the next foot bridge. After you get off the foot bridge continue south into the southern chamber and turn west. Head west until you reach the far side of the building, at which point you will emerge into the street. Be careful, however: While you are heading west you should run into another Russian patrol along the catwalk. Take them out when you see them.

The southern passage will take you into this building. Be prepared for the first two Russian patrols you run into inside.

Upon reaching the outside, continue to the south and you should see a burning tank. Pass the tank and you will come to a patrolling Russian tank and several Russian foot patrols. Take out the tank first, then slowly take out the Russian patrols. Once all of the Russians in this area of the courtyard in front of Nikoiskaya Tower have been taken out, you will complete this objective.

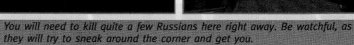

You will need to kill quite a few Russians here right away. Be watchful, as they will try to sneak around the corner and get you.

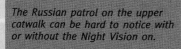

The Russian patrol on the upper catwalk can be hard to notice with or without the Night Vision on.

TAKE SPASSKAYA TOWER

From the courtyard in front of Nikoiskaya Tower, proceed west and you should immediately run into another Russian tank. Take out this tank, then continue west and take out the Russian patrols that are near you. When you get approximately half way through the courtyard you will run into another tank.

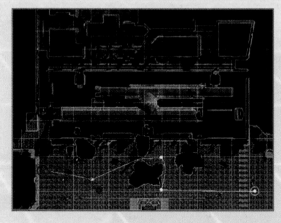

After you have taken out the second tank and its escort, be prepared for Russians coming at you from two different directions.

When you reach the far side of the courtyard and have taken out all of the Russian soldiers here the mission, and the game, will end. Sit back and enjoy the final images; you've earned it.

Take out the third Russian tank, then proceed west and take out the remaining Russian soldiers on your way toward Spasskaya Tower. It is important that after the third Russian tank you proceed with care. Instead of standing in the open, many of the Russian soldiers will be in bunkers with fixed machine guns. Your Sniper will prove incredibly important in allowing you to pick them off from a distance.

After taking out the second tank and the two Russian patrols that come at you, continue forward and you will be confronted by the third and final tank.

Right next to the now-defunct third Russian tank is a Russian bunker.

Now that the three tanks have been taken out, as well as the Russian patrols, you will need to clean out the Russian soldiers who are hiding in bunkers.

CHAPTER 6
Recon and Firefight Tips

CHAPTER 6
Recon and Firefight Tips

By this time you have had the chance not only to garner quite a bit of book knowledge but you have also had the chance to put that to the test throughout the campaign and, if you have played it to its logical conclusion, then you have made the world safer for those who enjoy freedom. Good job. So what now? Well, in order to satisfy that urge, Ghost Recon has provided a couple variations on the campaign missions, allowing you to play through them again without having it be repetitive by changing the objectives and the enemy locations.

The two types of mission variations that you will encounter here are Recon and Firefight. In Recon your objective will be to get from point A to point B. In Firefight, however, your objective is to clear out the entire mission field. Each is at one extreme, with the Campaign missions being right smack dab in the middle.

Even though you are a seasoned combat veteran, you will not have to go this alone. These tips will not be as comprehensive as the previous walkthrough, but they do not need to be. The following is a rundown of each of the variations of each of the missions, pointing out the differences between them and often focusing on a quick rundown of the easiest way to complete each. When there is no real easy way to complete a mission, more pointers are given. Exact enemy locations are somewhat random, but these tips address the locations where Russians generally patrol. As a result, you may occasionally need to modify your strategy. This section is meant to give the reader some general guidelines how to best complete these areas.

To ensure that you have as much information as possible, maps have been included for each of the variations for each mission. The Firefight maps often use the Recon map as the first portion of the map. Ensure that when the Firefight map starts off at a different location, than the position where you started, that you follow the Recon map to complete the first portion of the journey

Enjoy the rest of the game, and sweep through these missions. Once you are done you should be battle-hardened to the point where you can take the action online, and face some real enemies.

RECON

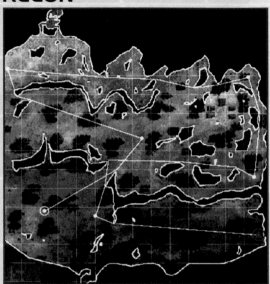

As you can see, each of the bunkers on this mission is empty, so you will not have to worry about Russians holed up inside them.

If you play this mission correctly, you should only need to deal with three or four Russian soldiers. As a result, you will need to keep quiet and move rather swiftly throughout the mission.

One of the safest and quickest ways through this mission involves heading north to the rock ledge near your initial position, taking out the Russian that you can see on the ledge above you. Turn west along the ledge and follow it as it bends and turns until you reach the Extraction Zone.

By doing this you will only have to deal with three or four Russian soldiers, namely the one on the ledge above where you begin, the second Sniper position that you would have to deal with on the Campaign version of this mission, and two more along the upper side of the ledge.

By taking out this Russian right off, you will save yourself the trouble of dealing with him later.

When you reach the smoke, simply run into it and you will complete the mission.

RECON

FIREFIGHT

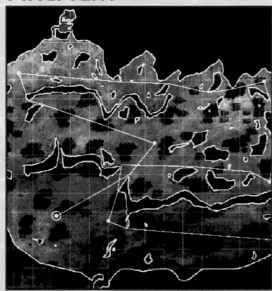

When you take out the first Russian on this mission, you will alert the rest and they will be ready for you.

When you are running along the upper area, make sure to look down and take out any Russians below every now and then.

While there is one Russian that is near the mouth of one of the caves, he will move out if you make enough noise near him, so you don't actually need to go into the caves.

As a firefight, this mission is a rather long run around with only one large battle. Proceed toward the first Sniper point and take out the Russians that are nearby. Upon firing your primary weapons, however, you will find that you will attract quite a few Russian soldiers. Take out everyone who comes toward you and, once the Russians stop advancing on your position, simply run around the map, using your Threat Indicator to sniff out their positions.

It is important to know that, unlike the Campaign version of this mission, the Russians will not be using the bunkers in the Firefight version. Instead they will be mobile and you will need to hunt them down.

RECON

RECON

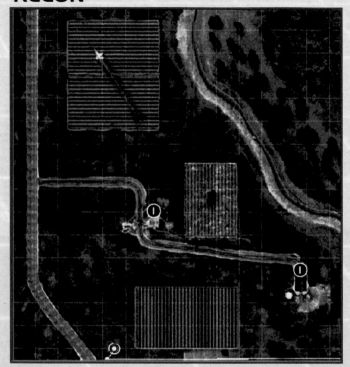

Avoid both the first Russian you pass as well as the patrol, and you should not face any more opposition along the way to the extraction point.

Unlike on the previous mission, Caves, you should not even have to fire a shot if you move quickly enough on this mission. To do this, simply begin by running east to the fence, then running south along it, through the stream, until you reach the far south side of the map.

During this initial stint you will pass one Russian soldier and a Russian patrol that was heading to your position, but if you manage to move quickly, you will not have to deal with them. Upon reaching the corner of the map, turn east. Next, run until you come to the smoke plumes, and you will complete this mission.

In the dark it can be rather hard to see the smoke, even with Night Vision.

FIREFIGHT

Like the Firefight on the previous mission, the Russians will be out in the open, and they will be mobile. As a result, don't count on many of them staying in the same place for long.

To complete this the easy way, however, proceed forward and take out the closest Russian soldier before continuing up onto the hill; take out the first three to four enemy patrols that come to you. After they have been dealt with, linger here for a bit and you will have two or three more advance on your position. Take them out.

When you are ready, proceed to the field in the center

of the map and fire a few shots to make sure that the Russians near you know where you are. Pick off whoever comes at you and you should clean up almost all of the remaining Russian soldiers. Afterward simply patrol the map, following your Threat Indicator, and you will complete the mission.

After taking out the first Russian on this map, all hell will break loose and you will be in the middle of a serious firefight.

Once the first firefight has been completed, you will find yourself standing over a Russian graveyard.

When the first enemy has been killed the others will, at first, attempt to sneak up on you.

RECON

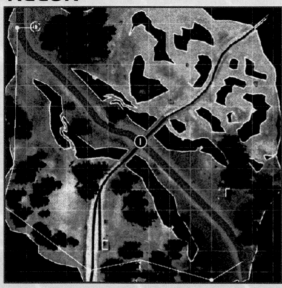

While it may seem tempting to just run down the center, it is important that you resist that temptation. Instead, begin by running southwest toward the cliff face behind the trees, then follow it as it bends northwest, then north, then northeast toward the extraction zone.

Along the route you will need to take care of three to four Russian soldiers, depending on whether or not you get caught by the second. The first one you will run into shortly after reaching the cliff face to the southwest, and the second you will come to shortly after crossing the railroad tracks. If you make too much noise taking out the second, another Russian near him will hear and come toward you.

The last enemy soldier is near the smoke indicating the end of this mission, and you will need to take him out before running for the Extraction Zone—otherwise he'll shoot you in the back. Unfortunately, however, he is rather hard to spot, as he is right next to both a bush and a tree.

Take out the first Russian soldier you come across, then proceed and take out the next two you encounter.

If you try to go straight for the Extraction Zone, you will find yourself riddled with bullets by Russians near it, even if you do make it past these two under the bridge.

FIREFIGHT

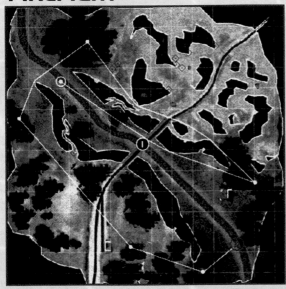

Begin this mission as if you were playing the Recon version, only take time to take out each of the enemies that you come across. Upon firing the first shot, however, you will bring several Russian patrols against your position. Take them out as they come at you, and then continue to proceed toward the extraction zone from the Recon version of this mission.

Once you reach what would be the extraction zone in the Recon version of this mission, proceed east, then southeast, then south, then southwest, going as far in each direction as you can before turning while following the lay of the land, until you return to where you started. When you reach the starting point, turn around and run right down the road, taking out any remaining Russians that you spot.

When you again reach what would have been the Extraction Zone in the Recon version of this mission, simply follow your Threat Indicator to take out any straggling enemies, and then finish the mission.

When you take out the first Russian here, you will not have quite as many come after you as when you took out the first Russian on the previous levels, but you will still have a few.

Make sure you get the patrol following along the eastern side of the map. If you are on the wrong side of a large rock formation, you may miss them and get shot in the back.

RECON

Unfortunately you will need to take out the Russians in each of the guard posts; however, they should not see or hear you coming.

Head west up the incline, then turn south by southwest and run to the cliff face. From here continue along the cliff to the west until you reach the road, then turn and follow the road north. Take out the Russian in the guard post before running across the bridge and taking out the guard in the guard post on the far side.

Once you are on the far side of the bridge, head north toward the hill, then follow around the hill to the west until you are facing north. Take out the Russian in the bushes, then continue toward the brink overlooking the river and run north along that, taking out another Russian along the way, until the pillar of smoke is to your west. When you see the pillar of smoke, run toward it to complete the mission.

Take this one out while he is still quite a ways away; fortunately the area is open here so you will have that opportunity.

FIREFIGHT

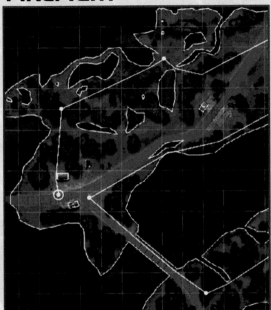

Begin this mission by taking out the Russian near you, then run up the incline and take out his friend there. Then, as with the last Firefight mission, continue as though it were a Recon mission, only kill each of the Russians that you come across.

When you reach what would have been the extraction zone in the Recon version of this mission, head into the ruins and take out the enemies there, then head to the northwest up the incline and proceed to take out any Russians near that point before turning west by southwest and taking out the Russians in the trees.

Upon returning to the dilapidated town near where you crossed the bridge, take out the remaining Russians and, if you still have not completed the mission, then use your Threat Indicator to find the remaining Russians. Kill them to end the mission.

Make sure you go through and take out the enemies in each of these buildings without putting yourself in too much risk.

RECON

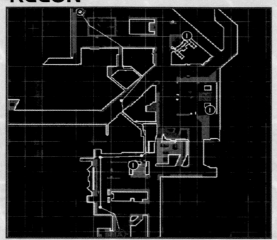

When you first start off you will have to kill the two Russians straight ahead, otherwise if they are alerted after you have moved out, you could find yourself boxed in.

Ascend the stairs here, then head to the west in order to get to cover.

It is quite easy to get to the extraction zone by running through the alleys rather than the open roads.

Make sure you don't forget the Russian who is near the extraction zone, or you could find yourself with a bullet in your back.

RECON

Unfortunately, you will have to tangle with far more Russians than you had in the past on a Recon mission here. To compound that problem, you will need to do it right away. When the mission begins, head north and take out the two Russians that are in front of you, then continue up against the building in front of you and turn west into the small walkway next to the incline in the road.

Take out the soldiers who are guarding the walkway, then turn and head up the steps and run west. When you are up against the building to the west, turn north along the walkway and take out the Russians along the path. Finally, when you cannot proceed west any longer, turn east and go behind the bank, then turn north into the alleyway.

From here simply proceed north, then when you get to the street head north into the next alley, and you will emerge near the extraction zone. You will have several Russians to take out along the way; however, once you reach the alleys you should be past the worst of it. When you reach the smoke, take out the Russian who is standing guard, then run into it to complete the mission.

FIREFIGHT

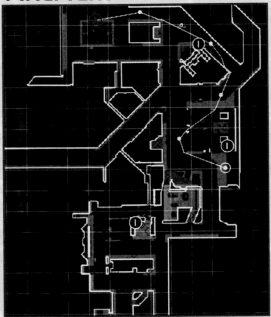

Be careful when you head through the garage, as there are a couple of Russian soldiers inside.

While you will have to tangle with several Russians inside the bank, you will fortunately not have to deal with any at the fixed machine guns.

Make sure that you are keeping constantly alert. Many of the Russians on this mission will come out from their hiding places and you may not see them until it is too late.

As with other Firefight missions, proceed in the beginning of this mission as if it were a Recon mission, only take the time to take out each and every Russian that you see, as well as the enemies inside the bank (and there are a couple). After you reach the point that was the extraction zone in the Recon mission, turn around and head east.

Proceed toward what was the extraction zone in the Campaign version of this mission. There will be one Russian on the top of the building as well as several on the ground. Take them all out and, if it does not indicate that you have completed the mission, use your Threat Indicator to root out the remaining Russians to complete the mission.

If you follow the two mapped routes and do not miss anyone, this soldier on the roof should be your last necessary kill.

RECON

RECON

If you make too much noise before coming to the first Russian that you will need to pass, he'll be joined by another Russian soldier.

You should be able to complete this mission without firing a single shot. While you will have to avoid several Russian soldiers, you will not actually have to shoot at them.

To do this, proceed west from your starting point until you reach the ledge of a cliff. From here proceed northeast along that ledge until you near a Russian officer. Walk slowly around the Russian soldier here, and continue to the northeast until you come to a rock wall.

If you make too much noise here, the first Russian you come across will be joined by a second. If this happens, simply wait and you should be able to pass both of them without getting spotted. Walk to the north around the rock wall and then resume your trek northeast. When you near the smoke, simply avoid the Russian who is guarding it and run for the smoke to complete your mission.

If you do need to take out the first Russian soldier, be careful— others will arrive quickly from across the road.

Be careful when you near the Extraction Zone; there is a Russian soldier guarding the area.

FIREFIGHT

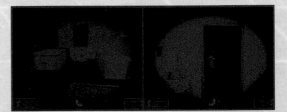

Make sure you explore inside all the structures in order to get all the Russians on this mission.

Head east and take out the Russian there, then turn around and take out his companion inside the house near where you start the mission. After that, proceed along the path that you would take if this were a Recon mission, only make sure to stop by the house at which you gathered intelligence during the Campaign version of this mission.

Upon reaching the Recon extraction zone, turn around and head west until you pass the castle, making sure to take out the Russian who is guarding the Campaign mission Extraction Zone. Next, turn southeast until you near the SAM site from the Campaign version of the mission and take out the Russian there.

Finally, turn around and head into the castle and take out the Russians within its walls, making sure to check the houses inside along with the ruins. When you are done, check your Threat Indicator and hunt down the remaining Russians.

In your first firefight, if you wait around long enough for the Russians to come to you, you may develop quite a pile of bodies.

Circle around the outside of the central castle at least once to ensure that you don't miss anyone who may be lurking there.

Many of your kills on this level will come from within the walls of the castle.

FIREFIGHT

RECON

RECON

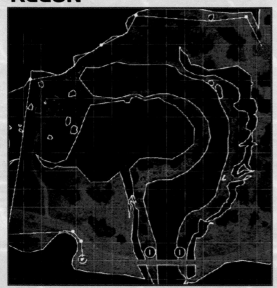

After crossing the water, you will want to walk as close to the water, and as far from the camp, as you can to avoid alerting the Russians.

You will need to take out a couple of the Russian soldiers along the ridge.

When heading away from the camp keep on alert, as there are several Russians on the other side of it.

Be careful when you are near the Extraction Zone. If you move fast enough you can make it in time; if not the Russian guarding it will shoot you.

Begin by proceeding northwest as far as you can, then turn west and take out any guards that you can see. Continue west as the ledge on your right slowly bends to the southwest, and continue to where you need to cross the river. When you cross the river, take care to proceed along the east side of the camp to the south. You will have to kill a few Russians along the way, however, so take care as you pass the camp in order not to alert any more to your presence than you must.

Once you are past the camp, continue south until you pass over the road, making sure to kill the two Russians along the way. Next turn west and proceed toward the extraction zone. If you make too much noise along the way, you will end up alerting one of the Russians near where you first cross the road, so make sure that you are quiet and do not stray too far into the trees there.

Upon reaching the extraction zone, either take out the Russian standing guard near it, or make a quick dash for the smoke. You should be able to make it there before he is aware of your presence.

FIREFIGHT

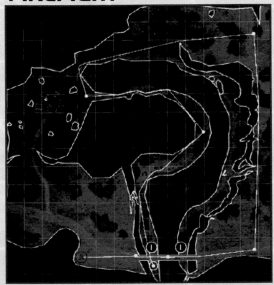

Because of the circular nature of this map, and the fact that the Russians will move around it quite a bit, especially when they hear a shot or two, you will have to circle the map several times in a spiral pattern to get them all.

By firing off a few shots, then waiting, you can get many of the Russians that come at you. However, because access from the lower areas to the upper areas, and vice versa, can be difficult, inevitably one or two of the enemy will always end up moving away from where they were, yet not quite making it to where you fired the shots.

While there may not be any tanks on the road as in the campaign version, you will certainly come across quite a few Russians.

Fortunately you should not have to go down both sides of the riverbank. Since you can see easily from one side to the other, you can clear both sides with only one sweep.

On your way to the Russian camp you will want to explore inland a bit more, so as to nail the Russians that were skipped in the Recon version of this mission.

It makes as much sense to start around the circle as if this were a Recon mission, then complete that and walk around the inner track, as it does to go in the other direction initially. The handiest thing that you will have on this mission is your Threat Indicator, because without it you would spend entirely too long going around in circles.

RECON

RECON

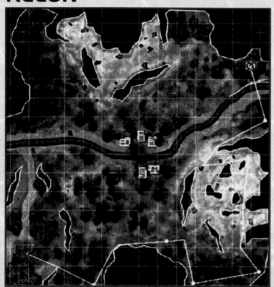

Be silent when you take out the second Russian soldier that you encounter in order to avoid having to take out the other who is near him.

If you are careful when nearing the smoke, the Russian guarding the road by it won't even notice you.

Begin by heading east by southeast until you come to a rock ledge. Nearby there will be a Russian soldier, but you should be able to ignore him if you are quiet enough. After you pass him, continue along the rock wall as it bends north, then east, then south, then east again.

Along the way you will have to take out one or two Russian soldiers, so dispatch them quickly and proceed. When you finally arrive at the southeast edge of the map, turn and head north until you are forced to go west. Until then you should not have to dispatch any more enemy soldiers, but when you turn west you will have to take out one.

Take him out quietly, then continue to follow the ledge as it bends around north and then back east again. Finally you will near a road where a Russian will be standing guard.

Sneak past the Russian and head for the extraction zone to end the mission.

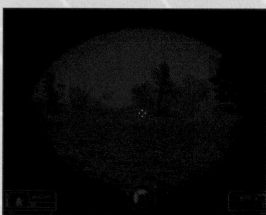

If you quietly pass by the first Russian soldier that you encounter on this mission, you should not be forced to kill him.

FIREFIGHT

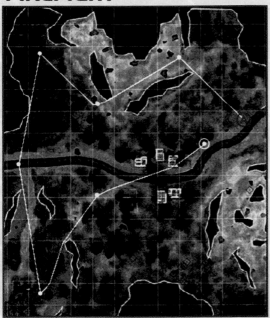

Upon taking out the second Russian soldier you will find yourself in a rather heavy firefight.

As with most Firefight missions this one is easily accomplished by beginning as if you were playing it as a Recon mission, only you will need to take out each Russian you come across. Watch out, however, when you take out the second because you will be attacked from the front, as well as from behind. In addition when you are on the upper ledge on the eastern side of the map stop and take the time to snipe down at any soldiers you see.

When you reach what would be the extraction zone in the Recon version of this mission simply continue around the map in a giant circular pattern, then when you return to where you started, forage into the center of the map using your threat indicator to pinpoint any Russians who are left alive to complete the mission.

When you head up the hill after the large firefight you will need to take out the Russian guarding the crest of the hill.

Be prepared to be ambushed by the occasional Russian patrol as you walk around the mission area.

FIREFIGHT

RECON

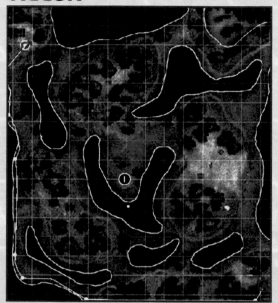

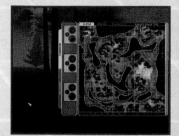

When you near the extraction zone be sure that you avoid the Russian who is guarding it and you should have no trouble reaching it.

If you pass him from enough of a distance you should not be forced into an altercation with the Russian who is in the marshy area on your way to the first island.

You will, on this mission, come near only three Russian soldiers, and of those only one will need to be killed if you approach the mission correctly. Begin by heading west along the edge of the map until you near the end of the island on which you start. Here you should be next to a Russian soldier. Take him out as, unfortunately, you will be unable to readily pass by him without alerting him.

Next, continue west until you are forced to turn northwest, and eventually north. While heading through the shallows you will pass one Russian, then you'll end up heading north for quite some time before passing a graveyard and eventually nearing the Extraction Zone.

When you finally do arrive at the extraction zone, simply walk up to it in order to end the mission. Take care to ensure that you do not tip off your presence to the Russian who is guarding it.

Regardless of how high your stealth rating is, the safest way to pass the first Russian guard is to take him out.

FIREFIGHT

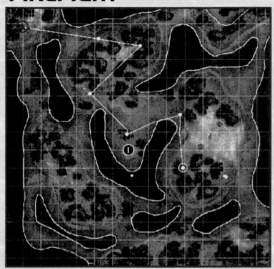

The water on this mission gives you a little more cover when you are walking through the marshlands, but when you fire a grenade into it a rather large splash will erupt that may hamper your vision.

If you make enough noise while taking out the Russians who are on the west side of the map, the rest should for the most part come to you, so you will only need to take out stragglers on the east side of the map.

Because of the way this mission is laid out, and the fact that the Russians will move quite a bit and attempt to intercept your forces, it really does not matter where you go. Instead, look at your Threat Indicator and head in the direction of one of the Russians near the center of the map, then make a lot of noise while taking them out. Afterward, the Russians will slowly advance on your position.

of the map by simply heading southeast after you reach the Recon Extraction Zone, then heading for the center island.

Whichever way you do choose to take this mission, just be prepared to take your enemies in squads instead of individually, because they will travel in packs.

Because there are so many Russian soldiers on the west side of the map, you will need to be careful when proceeding so that they don't see you.

Take out each Russian as they come at you, but also proceed forward so that any of the enemy who are far away from your position will hear as you get closer. If you do start this mission as if it was a Recon mission, you should be able to take out all of the Russians without even having to cross over to the eastern half

If you are unable to make enough noise, you may have to take out several Russians who are holed up in the house in the center of the map.

RECON

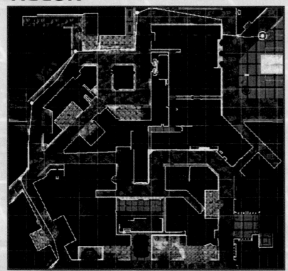

If you exercise enough caution and keep silent, providing you have not made too much noise when taking out the first two Russians, you should be able to slip past the third and fourth with ease.

Proceed northeast down the street that you start on. Once you are able, turn north by northwest down a side street. Shortly after turning you will come upon a Russian soldier surrounded by rubble. Since you will have to pass very close to him, it is necessary to take him out.

Be careful when you take out this Russian that you don't make too much noise or you will find yourself under fire from further ahead.

After the Russian has been dealt with continue north by northeast and take out the next Russian soldier that you see. Next turn north and follow the road up. When you come to the northeast turn you will see another enemy; if you are quiet enough you will be able to pass him without killing him, but if you doubt your ability, then it is best to take him out. Afterward, continue to the northeast and either take out the Russian near the downed helicopter or simply sneak around him.

Next turn east and go as far as you can, then turn north and go as far as you can, then turn east again and take out the Russian guarding here. Continue east, and when you enter the courtyard, simply head to the extraction zone to end the mission.

The second Russian should be easy to take out unless some noise was made taking out the first Russian, in which case you will have to approach with caution.

FIREFIGHT

There won't be too many Russians to worry about near what is the Extraction Zone in the Recon version, but there will be a couple.

Be extremely cautious any time you need to pass by a structure. On occasion a Russian may be hiding inside.

Unfortunately, on the Firefight version of this mission the Russian soldiers will move around quite a bit, and not only will you be confined to streets but you will also have to hunt through numerous back alleys and even some buildings. As a result there is no definitive way to go through this mission, because even when you clear an area, chances are the Russians will end up moving back into it when you leave.

You may choose to start this as a Recon mission, killing each Russian you approach, then complete the circle and return to where you started before heading into the center of the map to use your Threat Indicator to find any remaining Russians. However, it is just as effective as using your Threat Indicator from the beginning to take each one of them out.

Use whichever you feel most comfortable with—just use extreme caution. The Russians could be set up in sniping positions almost anywhere on the mission, and you will need to keep your eye out for them constantly.

While you may be able to clear the streets pretty quickly, most of the more difficult action will come when you try to clear out the alleys.

RECON

You will need to take out the Russian near entrance 2 in order to make it through the door without being shot at.

Once you manage to exit the compound there will be another Russian guard directly to the south of your position. You will need to deal with him or he will put a bullet in your back.

Be careful while heading around the walls of the POW Camp, lest you run afoul of the occasional Russian patrol.

While you may wish to take out the searchlight here, there is little reason to actually eliminate the Russian underneath it so long as you are quiet.

When you reach the extraction zone, make sure that you take out both of the Russian soldiers.

Once the mission begins head east, take out the Russian guard standing there, then proceed through the door and up the stairs, then down the other side and out the exterior door. Out here you will have one enemy to the south of you, so cap him before proceeding east to the edge of the compound. Turn and head south.

Along the way you should have to take out one Russian immediately after rounding the corner, so be careful. In addition, you may wish to take out the spotlight. Next, head to the southeastern corner of the base and take out the soldier there, then turn west and take out the searchlight at the far western edge of the base, then proceed north toward the extraction zone.

You will pass another searchlight, and since a Russian is underneath it, you may wish to take it out. You can ignore the Russian there once it is out, if you wish. When you approach the Extraction Zone you will find two Russians guarding it, so take them out and proceed into the smoke to complete the mission.

FIREFIGHT

This mission will truly be a firefight; one large firefight. You should not need to go outside the compound; instead you will simply need to move from one area within the compound to another, taking out enemies in each.

You will need to make sure, however, that you are almost always in a defensive position, and that you search each building. While some of the Russians do start outside the compound, you should not need to go out. Once the gunfire starts, they should slowly come into the compound. As a result, you will need to constantly watch the entrances to the compound and refrain from leaving your back to any.

One of the best places to sit is outside the door that leads from one half of the compound to the other. The Russians will pour through that door over time and you will be able to take out quite a few without even moving. If you do this, however, remember to look to your sides and your back to make sure that nobody has snuck up on you.

You will rack up quite a few kills if you just sit down and snipe Russians coming through the choke points on this mission.

Be careful when passing the various buildings. Sometimes one or two Russian soldiers may pile out and nab you.

If you have cleared out the entire compound and there is still a Russian or two left, leave the compound and make one sweep around the outside to pick up the stragglers.

RECON

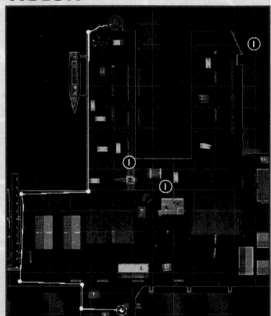

Unfortunately it is nearly impossible to slip by this Russian soldier without alerting him, and the best way to proceed is to eliminate him.

With just a little bit of stealth, you should be able to slip by this Russian soldier with ease.

Once you near the fuel depot you will come within sight of the extraction zone. Head into the smoke without alerting the nearby Russian.

If played correctly, you should only have to approach dangerously close to two Russian soldiers, and of those only one will require killing. To do this, however, you will want to avoid the straight-on approach and instead head up the incline.

Next go south alongside the small destroyer on the west side of the dock, while avoiding the area near the barge to the east. After a while you will be able to turn to the west. When you do you will come upon a Russian; pass by him very carefully, staying to the

northern end of the west bend. When you can safely do so, head toward the southern end of the ledge while heading west.

Once you get near the sub pen you will see another Russian soldier. Take him out, then turn south and go until you come to the wall. From here simply proceed to the east until you reach the Extraction Zone. Run into the smoke without getting too close to the Russian who is inside the building there, and you will complete the mission.

FIREFIGHT

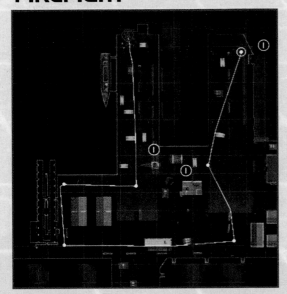

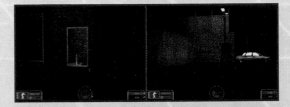

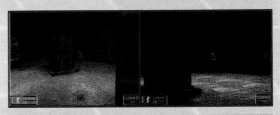

Don't pass too carelessly around the guard posts or you will find yourself shot in the back.

You can begin this mission as a Recon mission and it works out quite well. Simply make sure to take out each Russian that you come across, and run through the warehouses when you come across them near the first sub pen that you pass.

Check each of the buildings out thoroughly. There are Russians hiding within many of them.

Once you reach the point that was the Extraction Zone in the Recon version of this map, proceed east, and while doing so ensure that you clear out the Russians near the fuel depot. Continue east and search out and destroy each Russian within the warehouses on the east end.

Take care when you explore the central compound, as the quarters are tight.

After that, proceed toward the building near the center of the map and walk through it room by room, taking

Don't forget to check out the ship that is just southwest of where you start; there should be a Russian or two on board waiting for you.

out the Russians inside, then proceed toward the building just south of sub pen 2. Kill the Russians guarding inside, then continue into sub pen 2 and clean it out. When you

are done, if there are any Russian soldiers left, simply walk through the mission field and take them out. When you nab the last of them, the mission will end.

RECON

RECON

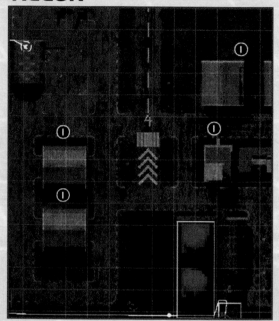

On this mission—if you do it correctly—you will only have to come close to one Russian soldier, the soldier who is guarding the extraction zone. Fortunately, you should not have to waste any bullets on him. In order to accomplish this, however, you will have to take the scenic route.

To start you will have to get to the opposite side of the fence to the west of your current position. This is accomplished by heading north through the gate, turning to the west and going as far as you can, then south until you are near where you started, but on the opposite side of the fence. Next head west to the far edge of the map, along the fence to the south.

When you reach the far edge of the map, turn north and run along the western fence. Eventually you will come to the hangar in which the Extraction Zone is

located. Continue north until you are just past the hangar, then turn east and run behind it.

Once you are behind the hangar, simply slip in and run to the smoke to complete the mission. While there is a Russian guard in the hanger near the extraction zone, he is on the far side and should not pose a problem unless you make too much noise.

Once the hangar is in sight you may wish to slow down and proceed with more caution, as you will not want to tip any Russians off to your presence.

If you get to the Extraction Zone fast enough, then the Russian on the far side of the smoke will not notice you.

You may ignore both the first Russian that you spot, as you enter the gate at the beginning of the mission, and the Russian you spot right before you enter the hanger. As long as you do not move too close to them, you should go unnoticed.

FIREFIGHT

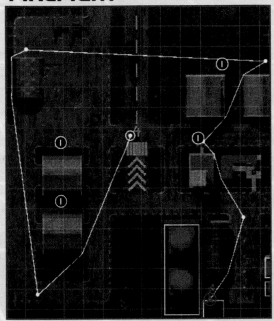

The Russian soldier in the southeast corner can be hard to see, but if you do spot him, he is alone and easy to take out.

Be careful inside the tower and the compound near it; you will occasionally be faced by more than one Russian in rather small quarters.

Don't forget to nail the Russian soldier between the two warehouses that you clean out.

Make sure to nail the two Russians that will be near you when you leave the hangers north of the tower; if you exit the western one too fast they may catch you by surprise.

When searching all of the warehouses on this mission, make sure that you search the second floor—there are Russians upstairs in each.

On this mission you will not have to encounter any serious firefights, but most of the enemies are rather spread out, so it will take some time to deal with them all. To start, proceed north through the gate and take out the Russian soldier directly in front of you. Then turn northeast and you will see a Russian to the southeast. Take him out, then continue toward the tower.

You will need to clean out both the tower and the compound near it, so take your time and go through each. Afterward go into the each of the hangers to the north of the tower and take out the Russian soldiers you find there. Look at your Threat Indicator regularly to make sure that you get all of the Russians in each of these facilities. Afterward head out and proceed west toward the hanger where the extraction zone for the Recon version of this mission was.

Take out the soldier to the north of it as well as the one inside the hanger, then turn south and you will come to two large hangers. Simply run into each of these and take out the Russians inside, and you should complete this mission. If there are any more Russians remaining, use your Threat Indicator to find them and take them out.

RECON

You will need to exercise extreme caution when trying to take out the Russian soldier on the road without alerting the one that is right next to him.

Remember to make sure that none of the Russian soldiers get away from you and alert others or have the chance to fire their gun if you accidentally alert them.

Begin by heading north toward the northern boundary of the map. Once you reach the northern boundary, turn to the east and continue along the rock wall there. Eventually it will force you to turn to the southeast, so follow it as it does but be careful around the first two Russian soldiers that you come across.

When you reach the end of the southeast projection in the rock, stop and look around. The third Russian that you come within sight of is to the north of you in a little alcove there. To get around him you will need to head due east; however, you will have to do so as silently as possible because he is extremely alert. Crouch down and proceed east, then take out the Russian soldier that you come to and turn southeast.

You will need to use extreme caution when passing the third Russian soldier on this map. He is extremely easy to tip off, and it makes too much noise to just shoot him.

Continue southeast until you pass under the pipes. At this point you should be on a road. There will be one Russian soldier right before a decline in the road, one to the east,

and another to the west. Ignore the ones to the east and west, but take out the one on the road and then continue down the road. When you near the camp you will have one more Russian soldier to take out, so dispatch him and then go to the Extraction Zone.

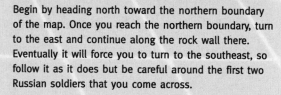

FIREFIGHT

Whenever possible, try to take out the enemy at a distance, since you will often find yourself with sparse cover if you get up close.

As with so many Firefight missions, it is quite practical to begin this mission as if it were a Recon mission, only take the time to kill each of the Russians whom you come across. Unlike other missions, however, you should not find yourself in a large firefight since, due to the lay of the land and the fact that the Russians tend to move around, you will most likely have to walk all over chasing down the enemy.

When you are ready, follow the path that you would if this were a Recon mission, but when you reach the camp turn and head west. Kill the Russians that you encounter along the way, but proceed until you can turn

northwest. Once you turn northwest you will need to go to a rock ledge, then turn west, then northeast once you are able.

Unlike on the Campaign version of this mission, you should not have much opposition when you encounter the house on the pass.

If you have been making enough noise heading up the mountain, you should encounter little or no resistance when you reach the top.

You should now find yourself moving into the inner circle on this map; continue until you come to a house. From the house turn south and walk up the incline. Continue to the top of the hill and take out any Russians up there. If, after this, you have not yet taken out all of the Russians, use your Threat Indicator to find the rest.

FIREFIGHT

RECON

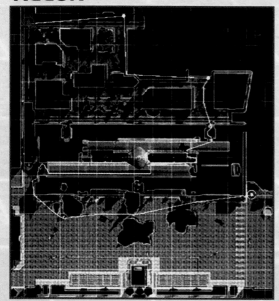

RECON

It can be easy to miss, but while you walk past the park, keep to the east and you should see the small tunnel.

When you walk into the long corridors, be sure to turn around to the east and take out the Russian standing there.

Upon finally reaching the smoke that indicates the Extraction Zone, you should not have to face any more Russian soldiers.

Unfortunately, due to the high number of Russian soldiers on this mission, it is nearly impossible to proceed without drawing attention to yourself. As a result, many of the Russians move around quite a bit, and you will need to use your judgment as to whom to kill and whom to spare, so for the most part Russian soldiers will not be mentioned in the following.

Don't make too much noise when you first start moving, as there is a Russian soldier right next to your starting position

In order to get through this mission, head east at the beginning and go as far as you can, then turn south when you may no longer go east. Head through the opening in the building that you come to and walk through the tunnel until you emerge at the other side. From here turn east and go, again, as far as you

can, then turn south and go through the opening in the building ahead of you.

Take out the Russian nearest you, then turn east and head up the stairs. Once you are up the stairs turn south and walk several paces, then turn west and walk until you come to a bridge to the south end of the room. Cross over the bridge and continue west until you emerge from the long corridor.

Be careful along the way, however, because you will need to take out a couple of Russian patrols. Finally, head south to the large courtyard, then proceed east toward the extraction zone. Along the way you will want to keep to the northern edge of the courtyard. When you reach the Extraction Zone, the mission will end.

FIREFIGHT

Fortunately, even in the large courtyard not all of the Russians are well-hidden; some still walk around in the open.

When you leave the long tunnels in the center of the map, be excruciatingly careful—quite a few Russians tend to come in at the last minute.

Remember to search each and every nook and cranny, since some of the Russians are rather hard to spot until it is too late.

For this mission you will not want to go in the direction that you did for the Recon mission, simply because you will miss too many Russian soldiers. Instead, shoot the Russian that is to the east of your starting position, then proceed to take the other Russians that converge on your position. After that go south, then turn and head west until you come to the second street that heads south. Turn onto the street, walk to the park, and turn east. Make sure there are no Russians here, then turn west and go as far west as you can.

Along the way you should have taken out approximately ten soldiers, so if you are low, go back and search for whoever you missed. Next continue south into the tunnel system and go for the stairs to the west of the entrance. Ascend the stairs and proceed to the southwestern end of the chambers here, taking out the Russian patrols that are scattered throughout the area.

When you finally reach the southwestern side, emerge and turn south toward the courtyard. Once you are in the courtyard, head east while killing each and

every Russian that you come across. After you have slaughtered them all the mission will end. If it turns out that you have missed one, simply use your Threat Indicator to hunt down the stragglers and round them up.

If you have finished all of the Campaign missions, the Recon missions, and the Firefight missions up to this one, then when it says you have completed the mission you will have completed them all. Get ready for multiplayer action!

CHAPTER 7
Multiplayer Examination

CHAPTER 7
Multiplayer Examination

The multiplayer portion of Ghost Recon has the same basics as the single-player game, but you'll have to adapt your tactics to accommodate the more intelligent, faster, and more accurate human opponents. For a more in-depth look at multiplayer strategies, check out Chapter 4. This chapter is dedicated to taking a brief look at the multiplayer environment and bringing up some of the most significant points of the various modes and maps. Each of the single-player maps can be played in multiplayer, with varying degrees of success. A quick look at the different types of multiplayer games follows, concluding with an examination of each of the maps.

 ## TYPES OF MULTIPLAYER

Co-op

This mode has the potential to be the most exciting as well as the most frustrating. Essentially you get a chance to play the campaign or quick missions with human teammates rather than AI controlled ones. While this can obviously add to the experience of Ghost Recon immensely, it can just as easily make the game horribly frustrating if the skill levels between the players are too different. If one player constantly rushes out into the enemy and gets a soldier killed, you may lose key team members far too early in a mission. We recommend only playing this mode with your personal friends, or at least ensuring before you start the mission that every player involved has a keen understanding of who is in command and how the team will be organized. Voice chat programs, such as Roger Wilco or TeamSound, while not officially suported by Ghost Recon, can help coordinate team efforts. f you use AI Backup in this mode, make sure that the unskilled players on the team do not kill all the AI soldiers accidentally.

Team

Team is where the true competition in Ghost Recon comes to light. Competitions between Ghost Recon clans, tribes, or guilds will put strategy and tactics to the ultimate test in Team multiplayer. While it is quite acceptable to try and play team games with total strangers in open multiplayer games, the minimum teamwork required to play effectively may make it intimidating if one player ends up on a team with a lot of new players and the other team is composed of Ghost Recon veterans. As in Co-op mode, a leadership hierarchy should be established before the mission begins, and each player should be informed of their role in order to ensure that the match isn't totally disorganized. Communication will matter immensely in this mode, so try to chat with your teammates often. Apart from that, as long as your team sticks modestly close together, you should have a chance. When all else fails, simply follow your team's best player and cover his or her back (but don't blow their cover).

Solo

The free-for-all nature of Solo multiplayer can make it both very exciting and very troublesome. On the plus side, you are presented with a plethora of targets and the action is usually fairly quick-moving. You also don't have to worry about an inferior teammate ruining your cover or disrupting your team's strategy. On the downside, you're always outnumbered and it's quite easy to be ganged up on and defeated by an informal partnership of enemy players. Since you're also playing alone, many of the cooperative team strategies and tactics in Ghost Recon will go unused.

 ## THE IMPORTANCE OF THE THREAT NDICATOR

The Threat Indicator, by default, on servers is left on. This allows players to fairly quickly locate enemy players on the map and makes the game a bit more speed oriented. Since you can never truly hide from your opponents when the Threat Indicator is on, there is a limit to how stealthy you can be. Combat in multiplayer Ghost Recon is usually brutal and quick with Threat Indicators on.

If the Threat Indicator goes off, this drastically alters how Ghost Recon multiplayer is played. With the Threat Indicator off, you will have absolutely no idea in what direction the enemy soldiers are, or of how close they are. On smaller maps, or maps with lots of players, this doesn't slow down gameplay very much, but once only one or two players are left, this can make the game tediously slow. Players can literally spend hours stalking each other on some of the larger maps.

Turning Threat Indicators off might be a good idea for the multiplayer-only maps, which are fairly small, but it is probably not a good idea for the campaign maps, which are fairly large.

MOI: CAVES

MOI Caves

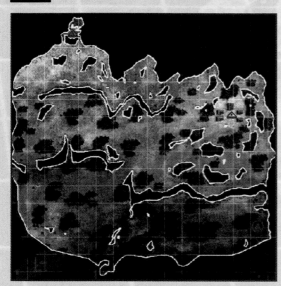

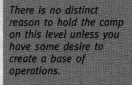

There is no distinct reason to hold the camp on this level unless you have some desire to create a base of operations.

The cover you find when playing Hamburger Hill on this map is extremely sparse.

This is one of the larger maps, but the overall design of the map makes it fairly balanced for multiplayer. The actual Caves on the map, for most multiplayer purposes, are relatively useless (unless you feel like camping in the caves). There are a few strategic points to be aware of, such as the fixed gun emplacement on the slope leading to the 2nd plateau.

The enemy camp on the far side is mostly there for decoration, but you can enter at least one of the tents and hide there if needed.

If you're playing Hamburger Hill mode on this map, you're not going to get much cover while you're king. The spot you must hold is almost totally out in the open; don't try to hold it for extended periods or you'll get sniped. If you are playing without Threat Indicators, and if your opponent is not very observant, then you may be able to get away with it, but it is still best not to risk holding the Hill.

The map is generally segregated into three elevation zones, each with a few access points leading to the next elevated area.

These points are generally stripped of cover and represent excellent defensive choke points. Watch out for enemy traps on these slopes between the elevation changes.

The fixed gun here can be used to catch an enemy off guard; just lie prone nearby, pop up, and take a few shots. Don't stay with the gun for too long, as it makes you a very visible target and you'll be sniped down once you reveal your location.

MO2 Farm

As you can see, you will have some cover on the Hill so see if you can hold it throughout the mission.

The upper windows in the house can provide you some sniping locations.

This map is so dark that even in the few lighted places it's almost always better to leave your Night Vision on. You may not find this map to be as balanced or as enjoyable as Mo1-Caves, mainly because the suitable terrain for cover is rather sparse and typically located in specific lines around the rivers and roads. The multitude of open fields and scattered underbrush leaves only a few options for sneaking across the map. If you're playing Hamburger Hill, however, you'll have a bit of cover while king.

The two buildings—a house and a barn—offer very little in tactical usefulness. The house is the better of the two, with several windows facing a couple of different directions. On the other hand, if you wish to take up sniping positions, the house as well as the barn may prove useful. If you do this, you will want to have ground troops near them so that enemy troops do not sneak in and shoot you from behind as you look out the windows.

If you want to throw your opponent off, hide near some of the more reflective rocks. They can resemble humans at long ranges, and you may be able to trick an opponent into shooting them and revealing their location.

MO2: FARM

While there is cover on the hill, you may wish to avoid the small structure there, as you will be a prime target for grenades in the closed quarters.

The rocky terrain on the east side is all-or-nothing in terms of cover due to the non-existent greenery.

MO3: RR BRIDGE

There are some ups and downs to the third campaign map when played in multiplayer. The center pass is almost totally devoid of cover, so it really isn't that great a place to hang around (unless you're a Sniper). The map is essentially cut in half by the pass, with the

two sides being joined by a railroad overpass. The railroad overpass can be used to cross between the two halves of the map quickly, but you are an easy target for nearly everyone on the map if you try it.

Avoid being down along the road for too long unless you want to find yourself riddled with bullets

The fixed gun by the building near the start doesn't offer much of a fire advantage unless you're trying to shoot someone on the bridge or someone trying to move down the center pass. If you stray to the left half of the map, you are greeted with a lot of trees and a lot of potential hiding places. The spot to control for Hamburger Hill

games is here, and it has a surprising amount of nearby cover.

The east side of the map is rather unusual. There are a few trees, but the majority of this side is composed of large rocks protruding from the ground. Players will be forced to dash between the rocks for cover, and peeking around the corners to take pot shots at enemies is quite applicable. If you can sneak past an enemy who is camping in the rocky area, you can outflank and make quick work of them.

MO4 Village

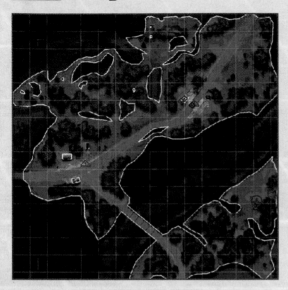

The buildings provide great cover for hiding; if you are trying to root someone out from them, take great care and go slowly.

The bridge acts more like a death trap on this mission than an actual means of getting from one side to the other. Avoid it whenever possible.

Be careful if you try to take the hill. Due to the sparse cover you will mostly be out in the open.

This is another very segmented map. The bridge that separates the smaller half of the map from the larger half is a massive choke point and just screams out to be watched by Snipers hungry for kills. As a result, it is

best to avoid the southern portion of the map, because chances are, most of the action will take place on the northern half, and if you are forced to cross the bridge you will likely wind up dead.

The smaller side of the map is mostly uneventful underbrush; the more interesting terrain is on the top half of the map. The few remaining buildings at the crossroads offer yet another sniper vantage of the bridge, as well as excellent vantages for

shooting at players camping in the buildings nearby.

If you venture up to the top rightmost part of the map, you'll find several ruined buildings that are essentially a battleground unto themselves. Due to the position of nearby hills and a low wall surrounding one of the ruins, the only real reason to enter these ruins is to do battle with other players hiding in them. The Hamburger Hill king location is a bit to the left of these ruins and is pretty much out in the open. If you're going to try and hold this spot for long, you'd better make sure that everyone nearby is dead. You best bet is to grab this spot early and then retreat and defend it from further incursion.

M05 Embassy

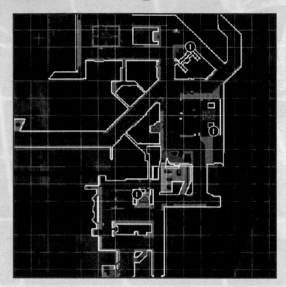

The garage offers quite a bit of cover, so you will need to take care if you decide to go inside.

Even more than most missions, you will be completely open if you try to hold the Hill.

If you decide to snipe from this location, it's best if you have a friendly soldier watch your back so that you don't get plugged from behind.

This map is entirely an urban warfare map. In general, it can be segmented into three sections, each with several streets, alleys, and sometimes buildings leading to the others. The first section, the bank, has several alleyways and a parking garage nearby that lead to the next area, the embassy.

The embassy in itself offers no real tactical advantage, but the walls surrounding it provide at least some cover for moving through the area. The Hamburger Hill king location is in this area, and it's basically a suicide mission to try and take it.

The last area, the helicopter crash site, has a building nearby that has a sniper vantage hidden up on the second story. This is a bit of a predictable spot for a Sniper to lay in wait, but it can catch an opponent off guard if he is not scanning the window for you.

Most of the cover comes from either cars or walls, so it's all-or-nothing cover for the majority of the map. Probably the most intense combat will surround the alleys and streets that link the sections of the map together, since they are likely to be the most trafficked areas. Battles inside the buildings, such as the bank, are likely, but the size of the map makes attempting

to hold or defend one of these buildings impractical unless you have quite a few players on each team.

M06 Castle

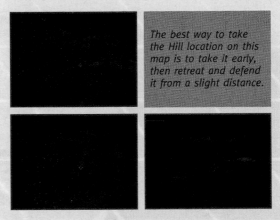

The best way to take the Hill location on this map is to take it early, then retreat and defend it from a slight distance.

As the name implies, the main terrain feature of this map is the decrypted castle which occupies a fair portion of the map. The mission is another night mission, so turn on your Night Vision goggles and leave them on. There is a machine gun nest just outside the castle in a slight depression, but the two fixed guns have almost no useful firing arcs, and it is otherwise a position not worth venturing near.

If you do get onto the walls, have a friendly soldier guard the way down so no one comes up after you.

The castle itself is on a slightly raised hill, so a slight cliff blocks access to the castle walls from some of the sides. The tree cover line does not extend to the castle walls in most cases, so you'll have to forgo any cover as you move from the forest up to the castle. There are several buildings scattered around outside the castle, but there are no real tactical advantages to any of them. The Hamburger Hill king

location is just inside the castle, but it is a hair's breadth outside of any useful cover.

You can take the spot for a few brief seconds, then retreat to nearby cover to pick off any would-be claimers of the hill. There is one slight sniper vantage on the castle walls, but with only one ramp leading up to it, it is a bit of a gamble to venture up to.

You can ignore the castle area entirely on this map if you choose to, but without the castle it is mostly a straightforward forest map with few terrain specialties.

It may look like an easy place to hold, but because you are at the bottom of a depression, you may find people shooting down on you from near the castle.

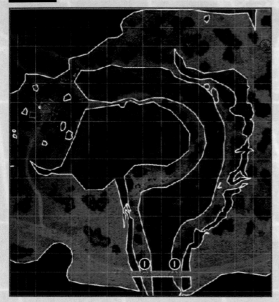

The bridge across the river offers almost no cover at all. It's an easy spot to defend, but a hard spot to attack.

The passes leading down to the river are narrow and open. Grenades or automatic weapons can clear them out easily.

You can use the hills in the lower-left portion of the map to get a Sniper vantage over the camp.

M07: RIVER

The heavy segmentation of this map's passable terrain creates several large choke points. With only light tree and underbrush cover for most parts of the map, there are a lot of predictable camping spots. One of the main choke points is the river crossing near the camp zone. This crossing can be easily defended by concealed troops from either side of the river.

The only other way to cross the river is to take the bridge, which offers no protection whatsoever from enemy fire. In either case, getting to the other side of the river can be quite a task. The Hamburger Hill spot is on one of two strips of land that run near the river. Each one of these strips has two small entrances that once again offer little in the way of cover

If you decide to cross here, make sure that you have secured the area.

for soldiers moving through. There is some cover for players trying to remain king, but the abundance of elevated terrain and the high visibility of the map mean that grenade launchers and Snipers will be able to easily pick them off.

It is best to try not to physically hold the Hill for long on this map, as you will find yourself dying often if you do.

The advantage on this map will probably go to the team or player that can maintain a stranglehold on the two river-crossing choke points. If someone is able to hold them both, the other team will find their movement severely restricted, and a pile of bodies will begin to form near the choke points.

M08 Battlefield

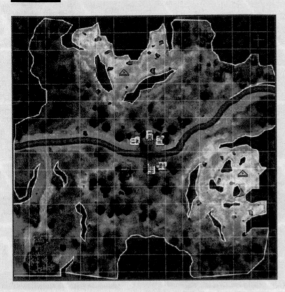

On this map you will have quite a bit of cover on the Hill; however, you will also be out in the open, so vigilance is necessary.

One of the better sniping spots on this map gives you quite a vantage point.

The place where you start in the Campaign version of this mission is a very secure location if you need to set up a small base.

A hollowed-out church provides a nice hiding place for evading enemy spying.

While it's not technically a night mission, the Battlefield is a dark map. Visibility is extremely limited and it's debatable whether or not it helps to use Night Vision. The main feature of this map is the series of ruins lining the road that crosses through the center of the map. The Hamburger Hill point is located in a crater near the ruined church, almost in the center of the map.

There is a large outcropping of rocks that extends from the bottom right corner of the map. This is a slightly elevated position, and it offers a partial view of the center ruins of the map. As a result, it is a prime

location for Snipers. If you are a Sniper, try to take it early and get someone to cover you. If, however, you are under fire from Snipers, scan this area first.

Near the bottom left of the map, there is a small set of ruined buildings, surrounded by plenty of

trees, that almost forms a mini-battlefield unto itself. Because of the amount of cover offered by these buildings, it can prove quite difficult to rout someone who is hiding inside them, so approach with caution.

The street and surrounding ruins are almost bare of cover. There are a few craters to hide in, and a few trees, but the closer you get to the center ruins the less cover you can find. There is an outer ring of trees that almost encircles the ruins, but it doesn't come very close to the street on most sides. The terrain makes shifts in elevation quite constant, and with the already low visibility, spotting an enemy may prove quite troublesome. Either stick to the trees or rocks on the outer fringes of the map or get into a building ruin or crater and stay hidden.

MO9 Swamp

Here is one of the low-lying waterways between the islands. Notice that they have a lot of cover, and any enemies that approach along them will also be partially submerged.

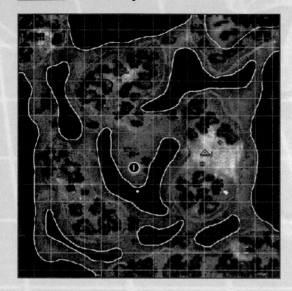

As shown here, some of the islands offer quite a bit of cover in which to hide yourself.

This is one of the easier positions to hold, simply because of the large amount of cover.

Immediately following the dreary Battlefield map, you get another low-visibility map. The Swamp is essentially several large islands with shallow waterways interconnecting them. The pathways leading to each island are actually rather small and represent the map's largest choke points. Unfortunately, because of the sheer number of them it will prove difficult to hold an entire island unless you have a rather large group of forces.

Typically there are two waterways leading to each island. There are several tents or huts on several of the islands, but most do not offer good vantages of any significant tactical points. The Hamburger Hill point is located in the center of the map, near a large house that sits by itself.

The house is a battleground unto itself. There is a small upstairs area, and the terrain

Usually there is a lot of available cover in the Swamp. Watch out for the occasional open area like this one.

below and around the house is extremely murky, with visibility so low you will need to rely a lot on your Threat Indicator to locate your foes. The amount of cover on the islands and waterways varies. Some of the islands offer a large amount of cover, while the others are fairly sparse.

The islands themselves are also fairly hilly, so find out where some of the noticeable elevation changes are and watch for enemies cresting their peaks. You probably won't need many Snipers on this map due to the low visibility, so stick with the faster-firing short-range weapons. It is good, however, if you can get one Sniper inside of the house, as he will have a rather large field of fire. This can prove especially useful on the Hamburger Hill version of this mission.

M10 Vilnius

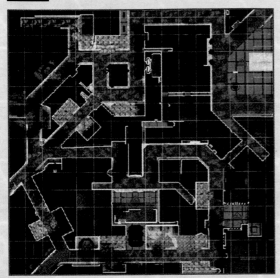

Be careful of Snipers hiding in the alleys on this mission as they can be difficult to spot.

Don't stay at the Hill for too long or you will be easy pickings for Snipers; the cover near the Hill offers far superior protection.

A sniper up in one of the dilapidated buildings can prove extremely deadly as they rain down bullets from above.

Continuing with the theme of dreary battlegrounds, Vilnius is a combination of the maps Battleground and Embassy. Visibility isn't as low as Swamp, but it is fairly poor. The entire map is set in a twisting urban landscape. Night vision helps a bit for spotting enemies amongst the rubble, but it also cripples your ability to scan the multitude of alleys and streets quickly. Several dead-end alleys and side streets line the map, offering snipers an easily defensible position to camp and pick off enemies walking down the streets.

While the tower in the center of this square can be difficult to hold, there are some bunkers with fixed machine guns here that can make this square rather easy to hold with a limited number of troops.

The streets themselves are almost entirely open, and offer very little in the way of cover. There are three large open areas on the map, each somewhat centered on a building. Some of the buildings are accessible by foot and offer elevated Sniper vantages.

The Hamburger Hill location is near the center of the map, just outside the main gates of one of the ruined buildings. It's out in the open, but there is some nearby cover if you're willing to give up being king for a bit.

Vilnius is a harsh map. There are quite a few ways to move between each area, and there is often very little cover when moving across the streets and alleys. The twisting nature of the map, combined with its poor

visibility, should result in close-range bloody battles. Teams will have to play it safe on this map, since the multitude of ambush points gives a big advantage to any team that is adept at laying traps. The map might be a bit too segmented for solo play, but teams should be able to play it well.

M10: VILNIUS

MII POW Camp

This is one of the easiest choke points to defend, because all you have to do is keep the door in your scopes and take out anyone who tries to come through.

From the vantage points that the choke points provide, you will be able to defend the base not only from the outside but also from the inside.

If you find yourself in the spotlights, shoot them out before someone shoots your lights out.

If you try to hold the Hill on this mission you will find yourself greatly exposed and near hiding places for enemy troops.

Another night mission, the POW Camp isn't one of the most balanced maps for multiplayer. The POW camp itself occupies a large portion of this map, and is broken down into several segments. The only way into and out of these segments is through a series of amazingly small choke points.

To make the problem of the choke points even worse, at each choke point there is a Sniper tower. Anyone holding the choke point from the inside will be able to take out anyone who comes near the choke point from outside the area, as well as anyone who may get close enough to try to enter the guard towers.

Given that the only way into and out of the POW camp is through these tiny choke points, you can expect nearly every player to amass near one of the gateways. The exterior of the POW Camp is pretty barren, with only a few scattered tree lines dotting the outer ridge of the map. There is a series of spotlights illuminating the exterior edges of the camp walls.

If the spotlights hit you, they'll follow you around for awhile, illuminating you for your enemies. You can shoot them out if you don't mind making some noise. The Hamburger Hill point is in the upper right segment of the map, near some portable buildings.

There isn't any immediate cover while you control the point, but you can quickly scramble to the nearby buildings for shelter if needed. The Hamburger Hill control point is also near one of the choke point gates, so you can simultaneously control the Hamburger Hill point and guard one of the choke points. Domination of this map will come to whichever team or player that maintains a stranglehold over the choke points.

M12 Docks

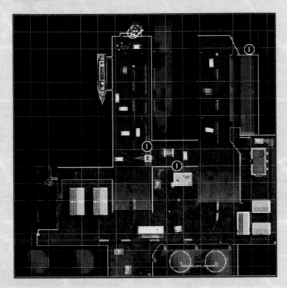

Despite the seeming advantage that the tower provides for defending the Hill, you will more than likely find yourself overly exposed.

Empty rooms like this will prove impossible to defend, and it is best to avoid them whenever possible.

Inside the eastern sub pen you will find quite a bit of cover, but much of it will benefit your enemies as much as it will benefit you.

While this is a night map, there are quite a few lights on Docks, making it one of the most illuminated night maps. Try to avoid getting yourself caught under the numerous streetlights. The Hamburger Hill point itself is located near the center of the map, right underneath a huge, well-illuminated Sniper tower.

You can try to scale the tower to get an elevation advantage, but in truth it will probably make it easier for enemies to spot you than vice versa. Cover on Docks mainly consists of scattered buildings and shipping crates. There isn't much in the way of partial cover, so stick to the crates and buildings and shy away from the numerous open areas.

There are many accessible buildings, but most are quite bare or have only a few crates in them.

The buildings almost all have two entrances as well, so if you duck inside one for cover, remember to watch both doorways for enemies trying to sneak up on you. The one exception to the plain building design is the large sub pen on the right side of the map. The inside of this sub pen is a twisted array of catwalks and furniture.

There isn't a huge tactical advantage to hiding in the large sub pen in most game types, but you can try to lead an enemy there and ambush them. Docks has promise to be a fairly fun multiplayer map. The map is relatively small and has fewer defensible zones than some of the other Campaign maps, so the action should be furious and fast.

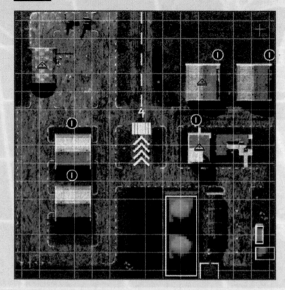

Unless you want to act as Sniper bait, it is best not to stay on the Hill for long at all.

Since the hangers provide more cover than the exterior terrain, you may find that they are a wonderful place from which to launch an ambush.

Providing one of the best vantage points in the entire game, the tower on this mission will prove far more useful in multiplayer than in single-player.

The Airbase is yet another night mission in the same vein as the previous mission, Docks. It's a lot like Docks in many ways: It's relatively small, has a lot of lights, and there are a lot of accessible buildings. The Hamburger Hill point is in a suicide location; don't

expect to be able to hold it for long. Instead of holding it directly it is better to take it, then retreat to the small obstacles near it and take out any enemy troops that come toward you.

Probably the main difference between Docks and Airbase is that while Docks has plenty of crates scattered across the open areas to provide cover, Airbase has relatively little in the way of cover between buildings. The majority of action will likely occur when a player

or team attempts to cross one of the open spaces between buildings and is spotted by their enemy. Apart from being ambushed out in the open, the rest of the combat will take place when two teams enter the same building. The largest building, the tower, has a high floor that offers a decent vantage of the surrounding terrain.

Apart from wrestling control of the tower from an enemy, you can venture into the hangars, which vary from being nearly empty to having a fair amount of unique terrain.

Airbase will probably end up playing out a lot like Docks, except that combat will be focused more around the buildings due to the lack of cover out on the streets and runways.

MI4 Mountain

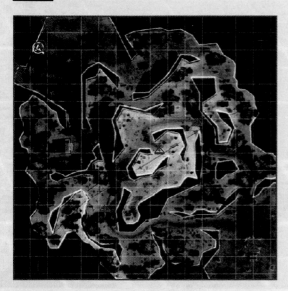

If you can imagine a cross between the first map, Caves, and the tenth map, Vilnius, you'll have a rough understanding of Mountain. It's a daytime mission and visibility is fairly high. As the name implies, the map is a gigantic mountain, with the peak rising in the center of the map. The Hamburger Hill point is on this peak near a small building.

Because this position is so low, it will be rather hard to defend, since people can easily shoot down into the camp.

A series of trails interconnect the starting points at the top-left and bottom-right of the map. The bottom-right starting point has several fixed machine guns facing the two roads that lead down to a series of tents and bunkers.

As your try to travel up the mountain, the road splits into paths leading to the right, left, and center. There are two middle-level plateaus on each side of the mountain's summit, one with several fixed machine guns facing an open field.

The cover here is more open than it appears, so be careful when trying to hold the Hill. You will be extremely susceptible to enemy fire.

While this position may appear better than the camp, it is in fact not— simply because enemy Snipers can easily mount the ridges nearby and snipe down into it.

The way the map is structured, there is at least one route that always leads past both fixed plateaus and the mountain summit on each side. This gives teams a large number of routes to use in attempting to flank the enemy. There is a large number of ridgelines that provide Sniper vantages for campers. Cover is bountiful: trees, rocks, underbrush, and the occasional building provide cover for soldiers trying to move up to the summit or to the other side of the map. Mountain is a big map, but it has a lot of multiplayer potential. The multiple flanking routes and sniper vantages offer many different points of attack and defense.

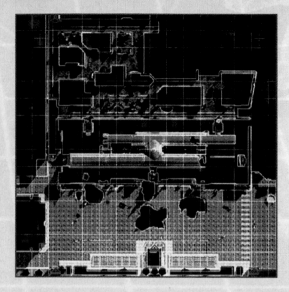

Red Square contains numerous ambush points and Sniper havens. It's a daytime mission with good visibility, and the terrain is almost all empty urban streets. There are essentially three main parts to the map: the northern district, the Red Square itself, and the hallways separating the two. The Hamburger Hill point is located in the top part of the map in an open field.

It is extremely easy to watch down this hall and pick off any soldiers that come down it.

Your best bet is to take quick grabs at the control point and retreat back to a nearby car or building for shelter. Between the top urban district and the Red Square lies a series of hallways and tunnels that must be crossed.

Anyone choosing to pass through this hallway will quickly become aware of just how easy it is to defend. Access to the hallway is limited to several stairwells, each in an open position that offers very little in the way of cover for anyone trying to pass through. If you do manage to make it down the hallway though, you can enter into Red Square, where another choke point awaits you at the exit.

Red Square is probably one of the most deadly places in the game to traverse because the sheer number of choke points and defensible positions that it offers.

Trying to hold this Hill is suicide without enough soldiers to watch all of the choke points that lead into this area.

Most of Red Square is open space scattered with ruble and the occasional fixed gun and bunker. Snipers on the far end of Red Square will have excellent vantages for sniping anyone trying to move down the field. Red Square is full of choke points and will be very dangerous for any team trying to advance through it.

CAMPAIGN MAP PICKS FOR MULTIPLAYER

Not all the campaign maps really have a great multiplayer feel to them. Some of them have multiple choke points, and others are so large and winding it becomes painful to try to find a target. If you want to know which maps we generally considered to be the best suited for fair multiplayer, here's a short list:

M01 Caves

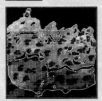

It's got lots of cover and has several flanking routes. There are a few choke points to defend but there's a lot of room to move about. It's a larger map, but should be especially fun in team battles.

M02 Farm

We don't rate this map as high on the fun factor as Mountain or Caves, but it's one of the few large nighttime maps. It's a bit of a toss-up between this map and Castle for best outdoor nighttime map, but Farm has more interesting terrain features.

M03 RRBridge

It's separated into three distinct paths, but there are a few ways to cross between each. RRBridge is a medium-sized map with a little bit of everything that doesn't favor defensive camping too much.

M08 Battlefield

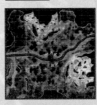

With its low visibility and crater-marked terrain, this map offers a lot of room to move but not a lot of cover. Battlefield has a very eerie feel to it and the low visibility adds a lot of tension.

M09 Swamp

If you're a fan of close range combat, Swamp is perfect. Low visibility and lots of cover means lots of brutal short-range firefights. This probably won't please Snipers at all, but for every other class it can be a lot of fun.

M12 Docks

Docks is yet another small map with modest visibility and a lot of cover. It plays out a lot like Swamp, but it isn't quite as limited by the low visibility and narrow pathways.

M14 Mountain

With multiple flanking routes, lots of Sniper vantages, and several fixed choke points, this map has a little bit of everything. It's a big map, so don't bring it up unless you've got at least six or so players on the server.

MULTIPLAYER

MPO1 River

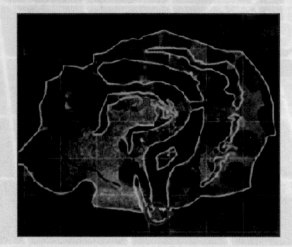

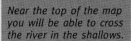

Near the top of the map you will be able to cross the river in the shallows.

Be careful if you try to cross in the middle, as you will be right in the center of the map and rather exposed; as a result you may find yourself acting like Sniper bait.

Don't confuse MP01 River with M07 River; the two are nothing alike. Whereas M07 River isn't a great map for multiplayer, MP01 is perhaps the best sharpshooter map. MP01 River is really quite small for a Ghost Recon map. If you've got more than ten or so players on your server, you may want to switch to a larger map. As the name suggests, River is divided by a small river that runs down the center of the map. The right side of the map is the smaller of the two and lacks any significant terrain features. Cover, in rock, bush, and tree format, is plentiful across the map. There are three distinct crossing points for the river. One spot is near the top of the map, near an abandoned house.

This house doesn't offer much in the way of Sniper vantage points, but you can hide in there to try to lose a pursuing enemy. The middle crossing is just below the foot of the hill, where the Hamburger Hill control point lies.

On the far bottom end is a small waterfall with a cave behind it. You can use the cave to cross the river, or you can hide in there and use the waterfall as cover to protect you while you snipe.

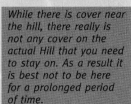

While there is cover near the hill, there really is not any cover on the actual Hill that you need to stay on. As a result it is best not to be here for a prolonged period of time.

The waterfall is probably the best crossing point, since it provides cover as you cross. You can hide out here and take out enemy soldiers that try to enter it if you like.

The left side of the map has a small hill where the Hamburger Hill point awaits. The control point is at the summit of the hill, and while it has some cover, there are at least three paths leading up to the summit.

You can control the Hamburger Hill point for a while if you quickly scan for anyone trying to sneak up the hill, but eventually someone will toss some grenades up on top, so try to keep your stays at the summit to a minimum. River is a very fast-paced map and is great for small, quick battles.

MP02 Night Battle

Because the fire near the chopper produces some light, you can hide near it and take out anyone who doesn't pick up on what you are doing.

You can also hide yourself a bit in the ruins near one of the fires. The added cover they provide also makes this preferable to the helicopter.

Since the Hill on this map is within a ruined building, you will have quite a bit of cover, making it preferable to stay on top of the Hill for as long as you can.

As the name implies, Night Battle takes place at night, with very few sources of light. It's an outdoor map, so there are no streetlights or houselights to intrude on the darkness. Only a handful of lights, such as the one emitted from the burning chopper, fill the void of night.

You'll have to leave your Night Vision goggles on all the time. Even with your goggles on, though, there are still several vision problems. The underlying terrain and many of the building walls do not reflect any light at all, so large patches of black obscure your vision as you approach a change in elevation or the dark side of a building. It is very easy to get disoriented and lost on Night Battle. The map is larger than River, but it is not as large as the command map hints. There are several destroyed buildings scattered around the map, some with fires burning on them.

Use the ruins as markers to determine where you are and where you are going. There's a lot of cover on this map, so the majority of your time will be spent simply scanning the darkness for enemy soldiers. Moving around quickly doesn't help you much; this map is heavily about remaining hidden while picking off your

enemy from out of sight. The Hamburger Hill point is located in the center of the map, almost in the middle of a ruined building.

If you can get under some cover while holding the control point, you should be able to defend your crown for quite some time before the enemy soldiers ferret you out of the darkness. Night Battle takes some getting used to; take it slow and try to memorize the significant terrain features so you aren't constantly getting lost.

MP03 Train Wreck

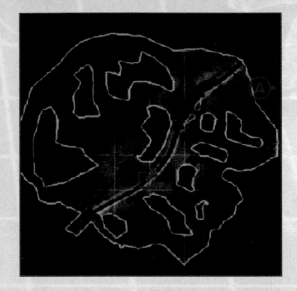

While it looks like it may prove useful from the outside, once you are inside the hut you will find that it does not provide a good vantage point for sniping.

Avoid attempting to make use of the fixed guns here. Their positioning will make them more of a liability than anything else.

The overturned train cars can provide a lot of cover, depending on your angle.

As with many of the maps, the Hill on this mission will leave you without any cover worth speaking of.

Creeping over this hill, you can get a safe view of the central area.

Train wreck is another small multiplayer map shaped somewhat like a circular arena. Visibility is modest, but most of the time it is not an issue. The landscape is pockmarked with several rocky outcroppings that will completely block lines of sight. Apart from these rocky outcroppings, there is a modicum of underbrush, a few wrecked train cars, and a small hut in which you can hide. The hut, however, doesn't offer a good vantage of any significant map positions.

There is one small central area along the train tracks that is fairly open in several directions. Two fixed guns are located here, but the guns mainly just face each other and are in themselves horrible positions to try to defend.

While you can occasionally pop up and use these guns, if you try to camp next to one, you'll quickly find that

the bunkers offer no real protection. The Hamburger Hill control point is right next to these fixed guns, and the only protection you can obtain while

controlling this point is if you are able to sneak into the nearby crater or hide prone near the tracks.

With a multitude of flanking routes encircling the central area, there is almost no single way to maintain a defensive stronghold on the map. Since sight lines are blocked for most parts of the map, Snipers will be at a disadvantage to soldiers using more potent short and medium-range weaponry.

MP04 Valley

Whenever possible, avoid the open areas of this map or you will quickly find yourself being turned into a corpse.

You can cut down on your number of blindsides by backing into a rock or corner.

The camp, while not offering a tremendously wonderful vantage point, does provide some cover if you have a sudden and urgent need of it.

While the Hamburger Hill point on this map lacks any real cover, there are covered places close enough to enable you to dash back and forth.

It is not a night mission, but rather a dusk mission. The lighting on this map can cause problems for players not used to it, because it blurs out shapes at a long distance but is still generally too bright to allow proper use of Night Vision goggles. This map feels like it should be easy to snipe on, but in actuality it is very hard to pick out targets at long range. It plays out more like a low-visibility map than a high-visibility map.

The terrain itself varies from location to location. Several places are crisscrossed with giant rock protrusions, much like the Train Wreck map. Some locations have plentiful cover, while others are totally barren.

Avoid these open areas like the plague—they're the few spots on the map where picking an enemy out at long range is easy. There is a deserted camp in the middle of the map, and you can use one of the tents as a hiding place.

It doesn't offer an excellent vantage, but it is a fixed location that is easy to memorize and fall back to. Near the camp is the Hamburger Hill point. While the point itself is quite devoid of cover, there are several

locations within a quick dash that can be used for cover.

The odd lighting of Valley makes it unique. No other map currently uses the same blurring light effect, so you'll have to practice on Valley if you want to adapt to it. Valley in a sense plays out a lot like a slightly larger Train Wreck.

MP04: VALLEY

MP05 Docks

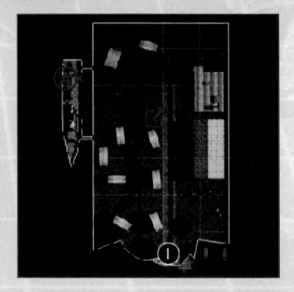

The buildings on this map are tactically useless. However, you may have to enter them in order to root out other players.

As with the crane on the Docks map, the crane on this map will leave you open to enemy fire.

Instead of sniping from the crane, try from the far end of the field. This way you can take out people along the ground as well as on the crane.

Inside one of the buildings, you can use a dead end room to set up a trap.

If you didn't get enough of the Campaign map Docks, or you just wanted a smaller, daytime version of the other Docks map, this multiplayer map answers your desires. While the map appears to be large, it is actually quite small. There is a large number of shipping crates of all sizes stacked all across the map. The Hamburger Hill location is located near three large crates, but you can't use the crates for cover while maintaining your crown.

There are two buildings off to the left side of the map,

In order to hold the Hill location, you will have to expose yourself near cover that could be used by enemy troops but is too far away to be useful to you.

but the only reason to enter these is to fight other players inside. They offer no vantages for attacking players outside the buildings, so avoid these unless you need a typically safe place to quickly retreat into.

A warship is docked off to the other side of the map, but like the buildings, it offers no real advantage to staying onboard, and actually traps you in a very confined position. Similarly, there is a large crane on the north end of the map. You can scale the crane and use it as a Sniper spot, but in return it makes you instantly open to attacks from nearly every other player on the map.

If you are looking for a better Sniper vantage on this cramped map, the central part of the map is actually one long barren area. If you set up camp at one end of the map, you'll have a nice vantage of everyone crossing the middle.

Docks, multiplayer version, has a lot of the same ups and downs as the campaign version. The combat is even more concentrated on short-range combat in the multiplayer version, and there is less area in which to hide. Use the large crates to limit the number of angles from which the enemy can approach you and take shots at enemies by peeking around corners wherever possible.

MP06 Castle

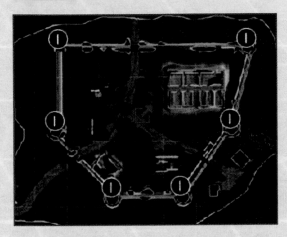

The rampart on top of the castle walls provides a great sniping location so long as no one comes up and nails you from the sides.

Trying to hold the Hill on this map will leave you wide open not only to ground fire but also to sniping from the rampart.

Even though one of the buildings does have windows that face the courtyard in the center of the map, its vantage point is not very good.

The special multiplayer version of the Castle map is another remake map like Docks. Multiplayer Castle takes the nighttime campaign map Castle and turns it into a smaller daytime version. The majority of the map is encompassed by a series of connected castle walls. While you can circle the castle from the outside, none none of the buildings outside the castle walls are accessible and there are no remarkable terrain features to speak of. Unless you are protecting a flank, or trying to flank another player, there is really very little reason to venture outside the castle. The walls themselves have an upper rampart that is accessible through the towers stationed along the walls. Once you get up onto the high ground, you have an excellent vantage of the courtyard below.

The ruins is probably the most defensible position in the mission. However, you will need to constantly watch the rampart above and your view of the courtyard will be severely hampered.

The walkway extends almost all the way around the castle, but a cave-in blocks the walkway at one point. There are many stairwells leading up to the walkway, so that enemy you just sniped from the rampart may respawn and try to sneak up behind you while you scan the courtyard for more targets. The Hamburger Hill control point is located in the central part of the map in a very indefensible position.

Nearly every player in the courtyard or up on the walls will have a clear shot of you if you try to hold the control point for very long. There are three buildings in the courtyard that are accessible, but only one of them has any windows facing the interior of the courtyard.

Lastly, there is a series of ruins in the courtyard that resemble a hedge maze. This is an excellent place to seek cover from enemies in the courtyard, but it does not protect you from all the snipers on the walls, nor does it offer you a very good vantage for attacking enemies in the courtyard.

The majority of the battles on Castle will consist of either guarding the entrances to the inner courtyard or controlling the upper sniper walkways. If you take the high road, watch for players trying to sneak up behind you. If you take the low road, watch out for Snipers overhead.

Note: This map must be downloaded and imported into Ghost Recon to be played.

TRAINING

Be careful that you don't get a hotfoot from someone down below when walking above.

While the Hill is somewhat defensible, you will find yourself open to grenades if you stay here for long.

If you just didn't get enough of the training base when you went through it and learned how to play Ghost Recon, you can come back and wage multiplayer

battles on it as well. The Training map really isn't that great a map to play on, but it is good for the occasional short-range gunfight. The map is

incredibly small and there are almost no open areas apart from some of the training exercises. A lower and an upper hallway encircle the entire base. If you can get into the upper hallway you can shoot out the windows at anyone in the open rooms outside. Or you can run along the training sections on the outside to avoid the point-blank interior combat.

Watch your step while you are in the upper hallway. The lower hallway has several grates that can be used to spy on or shoot at players in the upper hallway.

Apart from the two hallways, there is also a small section of the base that is pitch black. It makes for a nice ambush point, since most players won't know to turn on their Night Vision goggles before they enter the darkened area. You can wait for them to open the door and just mow them down as they enter.

The Hamburger Hill control point is located in the lower area where you learned how to control your soldiers via the command map. There are a couple of barricades you can hide behind while king, but you are very vulnerable to grenade fire.

Even though you can shoot down from the upper windows, your vantage point will be severely limited, so you will need to watch your sides to make sure no one sneaks up on you.

If you wish to set a trap, the dark area of this mission is probably the best point, simply because unaware players may find themselves initially blinded upon entering.

There are a lot of doors and narrow hallways on this map, so don't bother trying to play a Sniper. Expect a lot of surprise encounters, as many players will get disoriented on this map and literally stumble into each other.

WEAPONS INFORMATION

MI6A2 WITH M203 GL

ACCURACY TABLE

	STATIONARY	SHUFFLING	WALKING	RUNNING
PRONE	7	50	450	450
CROUCH	10	80	120	800
STAND	15	37.5	60	600

KILL POWER

HEAD	99%	LOWER ARM	44%
CHEST	94%	UPPER LEG	72%
ABDOMEN	77%	LOWER LEG	55%
UPPER ARM	61%		

ZOOM	2X
MUZZLE FLASH SCALE	2.0
MAGAZINE CAPACITY	30 ROUNDS

FIRE MODES & ROF

SINGLE SHOT	ROF 700
3 ROUND BURST	ROF 700

RECOIL
40

STABILIZATION TIME
.25 SECONDS

MAXIMUM RANGE
475 m

WEIGHT
4.76 kg

MI6A2 WITHOUT M203 GL

ACCURACY TABLE

	STATIONARY	SHUFFLING	WALKING	RUNNING
PRONE	5	45	400	400
CROUCH	8	60	100	750
STAND	10	80	50	500

KILL POWER

HEAD	99%	LOWER ARM	44%
CHEST	94%	UPPER LEG	72%
ABDOMEN	77%	LOWER LEG	55%
UPPER ARM	61%		

ZOOM	2X
MUZZLE FLASH SCALE	2.0
MAGAZINE CAPACITY	30 ROUNDS

FIRE MODES & ROF

SINGLE SHOT	ROF 700
3 ROUND BURST	ROF 700

RECOIL
50

STABILIZATION TIME
.2 SECONDS

MAXIMUM RANGE
475 m

WEIGHT
3.4 kg

OICW WITH GL

ACCURACY TABLE

	STATIONARY	SHUFFLING	WALKING	RUNNING
PRONE	4	45	350	350
CROUCH	8	55	200	900
STAND	10	35	60	600

KILL POWER

HEAD	99%	LOWER ARM	44%
CHEST	94%	UPPER LEG	72%
ABDOMEN	77%	LOWER LEG	55%
UPPER ARM	61%		

ZOOM	3X
MUZZLE FLASH SCALE	1.5
MAGAZINE CAPACITY	30 ROUNDS

FIRE MODES & ROF

SINGLE SHOT	ROF 750
3 ROUND BURST	ROF 750
FULL AUTO	ROF 775

RECOIL
42

STABILIZATION TIME
.2 SECONDS

MAXIMUM RANGE
475 m

WEIGHT
5 kg

OICW WITHOUT GL

ACCURACY TABLE

	STATIONARY	SHUFFLING	WALKING	RUNNING
PRONE	3	45	300	300
CROUCH	5	50	175	800
STAND	8	32	48	560

KILL POWER

HEAD	99%	LOWER ARM	44%
CHEST	94%	UPPER LEG	72%
ABDOMEN	77%	LOWER LEG	55%
UPPER ARM	61%		

ZOOM	5X
MUZZLE FLASH SCALE	1.5
MAGAZINE CAPACITY	30 ROUNDS

FIRE MODES & ROF

SINGLE SHOT	ROF 750
3 ROUND BURST	ROF 750
FULL AUTO	ROF 775

RECOIL
50

STABILIZATION TIME
.175 SECONDS

MAXIMUM RANGE
475 m

WEIGHT
5 kg

CARBINES

M4

ACCURACY TABLE

	STATIONARY	SHUFFLING	WALKING	RUNNING
PRONE	8	65	250	250
CROUCH	10	80	110	650
STAND	15	45	60	525

KILL POWER

HEAD	99%	LOWER ARM	44%
CHEST	94%	UPPER LEG	72%
ABDOMEN	77%	LOWER LEG	55%
UPPER ARM	61%		

ZOOM	2X
MUZZLE FLASH SCALE	1.5
MAGAZINE CAPACITY	30 ROUNDS

FIRE MODES & ROF

SINGLE SHOT	ROF 750
FULL AUTO	ROF 750

RECOIL
53

STABILIZATION TIME
.15 SECONDS

MAXIMUM RANGE
475 m

WEIGHT
2.54 kg

SA-80

ACCURACY TABLE

	STATIONARY	SHUFFLING	WALKING	RUNNING
PRONE	8	55	300	300
CROUCH	10	65	120	750
STAND	15	45	60	525

KILL POWER

HEAD	99%	LOWER ARM	44%
CHEST	94%	UPPER LEG	72%
ABDOMEN	77%	LOWER LEG	55%
UPPER ARM	61%		

ZOOM	3X
MUZZLE FLASH SCALE	1.5
MAGAZINE CAPACITY	30 ROUNDS

FIRE MODES & ROF

SINGLE SHOT	ROF 775
FULL AUTO	ROF 775

RECOIL
53

STABILIZATION TIME
.125 SECONDS

MAXIMUM RANGE
475 m

WEIGHT
3.71 kg

LIGHT MACHINE GUNS

M249 SAW

ACCURACY TABLE

	STATIONARY	SHUFFLING	WALKING	RUNNING
PRONE	5	70	500	500
CROUCH	20	80	300	1200
STAND	40	60	240	1000

KILL POWER

HEAD	99%	LOWER ARM	44%
CHEST	94%	UPPER LEG	72%
ABDOMEN	77%	LOWER LEG	55%
UPPER ARM	61%		

ZOOM	2X
MUZZLE FLASH SCALE	2.5
MAGAZINE CAPACITY	200 ROUNDS

FIRE MODES & ROF
FULL AUTO   ROF 750

RECOIL
40

STABILIZATION TIME
.25 SECONDS

MAXIMUM RANGE
475 m

WEIGHT
7.03 kg

MG3

ACCURACY TABLE

	STATIONARY	SHUFFLING	WALKING	RUNNING
PRONE	5	75	300	300
CROUCH	15	80	275	1600
STAND	25	56	245	1400

KILL POWER

HEAD	99%	LOWER ARM	56%
CHEST	95%	UPPER LEG	78%
ABDOMEN	82%	LOWER LEG	65%
UPPER ARM	69%		

ZOOM	2X
MUZZLE FLASH SCALE	3.0
MAGAZINE CAPACITY	100 ROUNDS

FIRE MODES & ROF
FULL AUTO   ROF 1300

RECOIL
30

STABILIZATION TIME
.25 SECONDS

MAXIMUM RANGE
475 m

WEIGHT
11.05 kg

RPK74

ACCURACY TABLE

	STATIONARY	SHUFFLING	WALKING	RUNNING
PRONE	5	60	450	450
CROUCH	20	90	250	1100
STAND	40	50	200	900

KILL POWER

HEAD	99%	LOWER ARM	41%
CHEST	94%	UPPER LEG	70%
ABDOMEN	76%	LOWER LEG	52%
UPPER ARM	58%		

ZOOM	2X
MUZZLE FLASH SCALE	2.75
MAGAZINE CAPACITY	75 ROUNDS

FIRE MODES & ROF

SINGLE SHOT	ROF 660
FULL AUTO	ROF 660

RECOIL
43

STABILIZATION TIME
.25 SECONDS

MAXIMUM RANGE
475 m

WEIGHT
5.0 kg

PISTOLS

M9

ACCURACY TABLE

	STATIONARY	SHUFFLING	WALKING	RUNNING
PRONE	10	50	200	200
CROUCH	15	65	150	650
STAND	30	60	70	600

KILL POWER

HEAD	97%	LOWER ARM	0%
CHEST	73%	UPPER LEG	0%
ABDOMEN	0%	LOWER LEG	0%
UPPER ARM	0%		

ZOOM	IX
MUZZLE FLASH SCALE	1.0
MAGAZINE CAPACITY	15 ROUNDS

FIRE MODES & ROF
SINGLE SHOT   ROF 600

RECOIL
100

STABILIZATION TIME
.25 SECONDS

MAXIMUM RANGE
246 m

WEIGHT
0.95 kg

M9-SD

ACCURACY TABLE

	STATIONARY	SHUFFLING	WALKING	RUNNING
PRONE	10	55	200	200
CROUCH	12	70	180	550
STAND	25	50	75	300

KILL POWER

HEAD	96%	LOWER ARM	0%
CHEST	61%	UPPER LEG	0%
ABDOMEN	0%	LOWER LEG	0%
UPPER ARM	0%		

ZOOM	IX
MUZZLE FLASH SCALE	.01 (SILENCED)
MAGAZINE CAPACITY	15 ROUNDS

FIRE MODES & ROF
SINGLE SHOT   ROF 600

RECOIL
90

STABILIZATION TIME
.275 SECONDS

MAXIMUM RANGE
246 m

WEIGHT
1.11 kg

WEAPONS INFORMATION

SNIPER RIFLES

M24

ACCURACY TABLE

	STATIONARY	SHUFFLING	WALKING	RUNNING
PRONE	.5	70	600	600
CROUCH	1	95	300	1500
STAND	2	46	120	1000

KILL POWER

HEAD	99%	LOWER ARM	56%
CHEST	95%	UPPER LEG	78%
ABDOMEN	82%	LOWER LEG	65%
UPPER ARM	69%		

ZOOM	5X
MUZZLE FLASH SCALE	3.0
MAGAZINE CAPACITY	6 ROUNDS

FIRE MODES & ROF
SINGLE SHOT   ROF 300

RECOIL
100

STABILIZATION TIME
.45 SECONDS

MAXIMUM RANGE
475 m

WEIGHT
6.284 kg

M82AI

ACCURACY TABLE

	STATIONARY	SHUFFLING	WALKING	RUNNING
PRONE	.5	20	300	300
CROUCH	2	60	200	1800
STAND	5	50	125	1500

KILL POWER

HEAD	99%	LOWER ARM	62%
CHEST	96%	UPPER LEG	81%
ABDOMEN	84%	LOWER LEG	69%
UPPER ARM	73%		

ZOOM	5X, 10X
MUZZLE FLASH SCALE	4.0
MAGAZINE CAPACITY	10 ROUNDS

FIRE MODES & ROF
SINGLE SHOT   ROF 300

RECOIL
100

STABILIZATION TIME
.65 SECONDS

MAXIMUM RANGE
481 m

WEIGHT
12.9 kg

SVD 'DRAGUNOV'

ACCURACY TABLE

	STATIONARY	SHUFFLING	WALKING	RUNNING
PRONE	1	50	350	350
CROUCH	5	140	400	3500
STAND	10	120	310	3000

KILL POWER

HEAD	99%	LOWER ARM	56%
CHEST	95%	UPPER LEG	78%
ABDOMEN	82%	LOWER LEG	65%
UPPER ARM	69%		

ZOOM	5X, 15X
MUZZLE FLASH SCALE	3.0
MAGAZINE CAPACITY	10 ROUNDS

FIRE MODES & ROF
SINGLE SHOT   ROF 300

RECOIL
110

STABILIZATION TIME
.4 SECONDS

MAXIMUM RANGE
500m

WEIGHT
4.3 kg

L96AI

ACCURACY TABLE

	STATIONARY	SHUFFLING	WALKING	RUNNING
PRONE	.75	70	500	600
CROUCH	2	90	200	1200
STAND	5	45	125	1000

KILL POWER

HEAD	99%	LOWER ARM	44%
CHEST	94%	UPPER LEG	72%
ABDOMEN	77%	LOWER LEG	55%
UPPER ARM	61%		

ZOOM	6X
MUZZLE FLASH SCALE	2.5
MAGAZINE CAPACITY	10 ROUNDS

FIRE MODES & ROF
SINGLE SHOT   ROF 300

RECOIL
75

STABILIZATION TIME
.5 SECONDS

MAXIMUM RANGE
475 m

WEIGHT
3.4 kg

WEAPONS INFORMATION

MP5

ACCURACY TABLE

	STATIONARY	SHUFFLING	WALKING	RUNNING
PRONE	8	55	200	200
CROUCH	15	70	180	550
STAND	25	50	75	300

KILL POWER

HEAD	96%	LOWER ARM	0%
CHEST	61%	UPPER LEG	0%
ABDOMEN	0%	LOWER LEG	0%
UPPER ARM	0%		

ZOOM	1.5X
MUZZLE FLASH SCALE	1.0
MAGAZINE CAPACITY	30 ROUNDS

FIRE MODES & ROF

SINGLE SHOT	ROF 800
3 ROUND BURST	ROF 800
FULL AUTO	ROF 800

RECOIL
53

STABILIZATION TIME
.125 SECONDS

MAXIMUM RANGE
220 m

WEIGHT
2.54 kg

MP5-SD

ACCURACY TABLE

	STATIONARY	SHUFFLING	WALKING	RUNNING
PRONE	8	50	350	350
CROUCH	10	60	200	650
STAND	20	40	60	400

KILL POWER

HEAD	99%	LOWER ARM	44%
CHEST	94%	UPPER LEG	72%
ABDOMEN	77%	LOWER LEG	55%
UPPER ARM	61%		

ZOOM	1.5X
MUZZLE FLASH SCALE	0.01 (SILENCED)
MAGAZINE CAPACITY	30 ROUNDS

FIRE MODES & ROF

SINGLE SHOT	ROF 700
3 ROUND BURST	ROF 700
FULL AUTO	ROF 700

RECOIL
50

STABILIZATION TIME
.15 SECONDS

MAXIMUM RANGE
475 m

WEIGHT
3.4 kg

EXPLOSIVES

M136 ANTI-TANK
ROCKET LAUNCHER

ACCURACY TABLE

	STATIONARY	SHUFFLING	WALKING	RUNNING
PRONE	1.5	50	300	300
CROUCH	2	60	150	700
STAND	4	40	100	500

KILL POWER

HEAD	99%	LOWER ARM	54%
CHEST	95%	UPPER LEG	77%
ABDOMEN	81%	LOWER LEG	63%
UPPER ARM	67%		

ZOOM	IX
MUZZLE FLASH SCALE	1.0
MAGAZINE CAPACITY	1 ROUND

FIRE MODES & ROF
SINGLE SHOT   ROF 600

BLAST RADIUS
10 m

RECOIL
1.5

STABILIZATION TIME
1 SECOND

MAXIMUM RANGE
188 m

M18 CLAYMORE MINE

BLAST RADIUS

SPECIAL

KILL POWER

HEAD	99%
CHEST	99%
ABDOMEN	97%
UPPER ARM	95%
LOWER ARM	93%
LOWER LEG	96%
UPPER LEG	94%

WEAPONS INFORMATION

M203 UNDERBARREL GRENADE LAUNCHER

ACCURACY TABLE

	STATIONARY	SHUFFLING	WALKING	RUNNING
PRONE	7	50	450	450
CROUCH	10	80	120	800
STAND	15	37.5	60	600

KILL POWER

HEAD	98%	LOWER ARM	0%
CHEST	88%	UPPER LEG	44%
ABDOMEN	55%	LOWER LEG	11%
UPPER ARM	22%		

ZOOM	IX
MUZZLE FLASH SCALE	0.0
MAGAZINE CAPACITY	1 ROUND

FIRE MODES & ROF
SINGLE SHOT   ROF 600

BLAST RADIUS
8 M

RECOIL
1.5

STABILIZATION TIME
.25 SECONDS

M67 HAND GRENADE

BLAST RADIUS

10 m (4 SECOND DELAY)

KILL POWER

HEAD	99%
CHEST	95%
ABDOMEN	81%
UPPER ARM	67%
LOWER ARM	54%
LOWER LEG	77%
UPPER LEG	63%

OICW GRENADE LAUNCHER

ACCURACY TABLE

	STATIONARY	SHUFFLING	WALKING	RUNNING
PRONE	4	45	350	350
CROUCH	8	55	200	900
STAND	10	35	600	650

KILL POWER

HEAD	98%	LOWER ARM	0%
CHEST	81%	UPPER LEG	7%
ABDOMEN	26%	LOWER LEG	0%
UPPER ARM	0%		

ZOOM	IX
MUZZLE FLASH SCALE	0.00001
MAGAZINE CAPACITY	6 ROUNDS

FIRE MODES & ROF
SINGLE SHOT   ROF 600

BLAST RADIUS
7 m

RECOIL
1.5

STABILIZATION TIME
1 SECOND

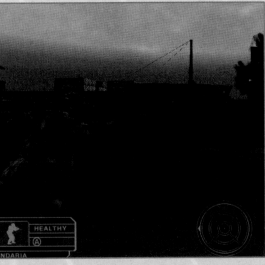

MP01 RIVER

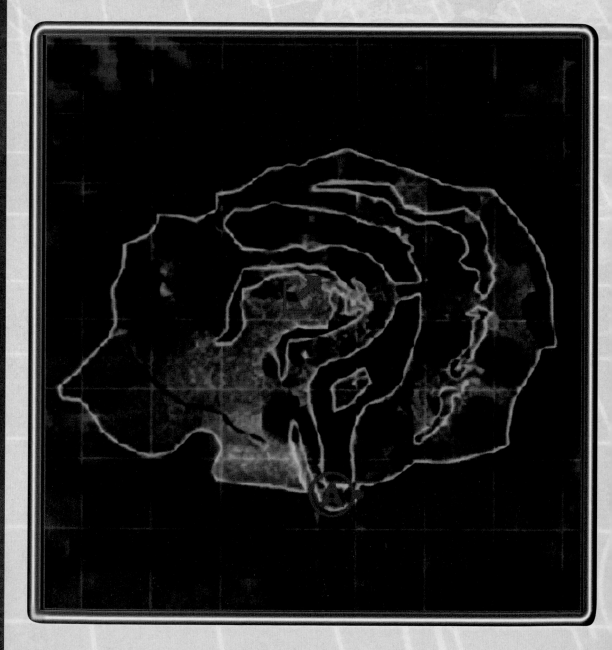

MP02 NIGHT BATTLE

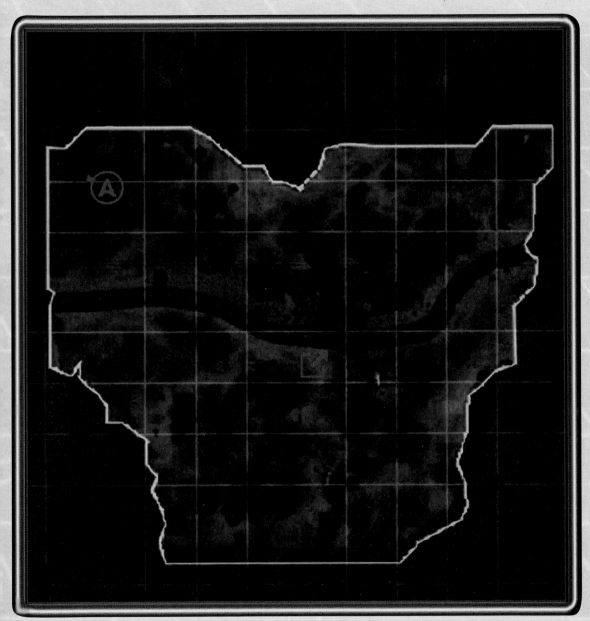

MP03 TRAIN WRECK

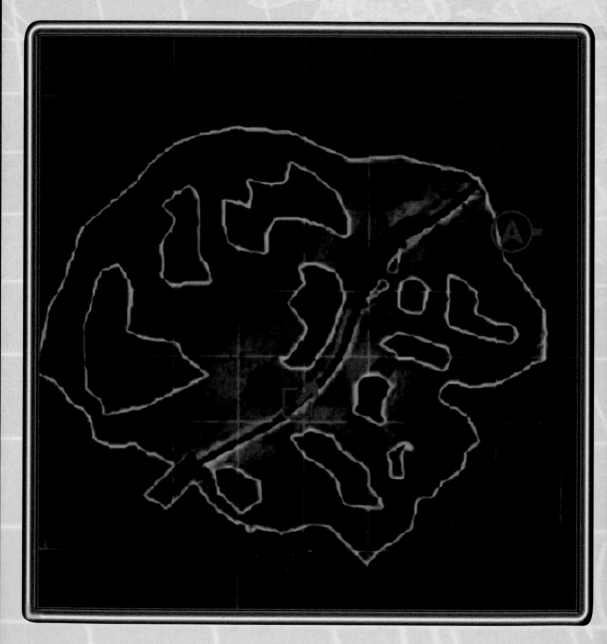

MP04 VALLEY

MP05 DOCKS

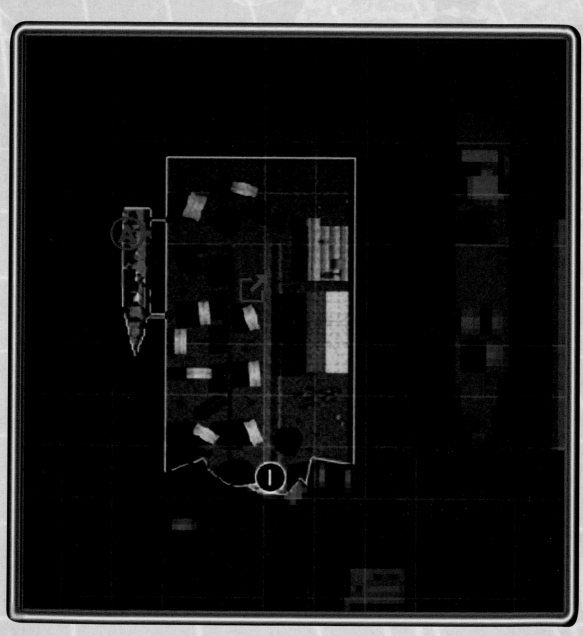

MP06 CASTLE

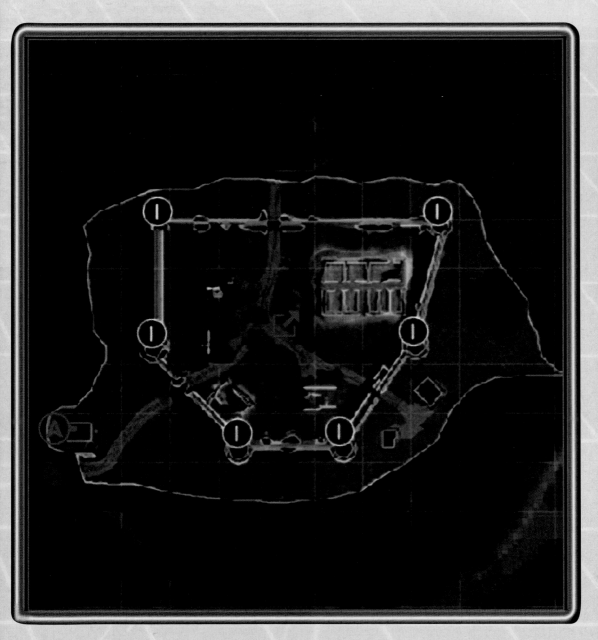

TRAINING

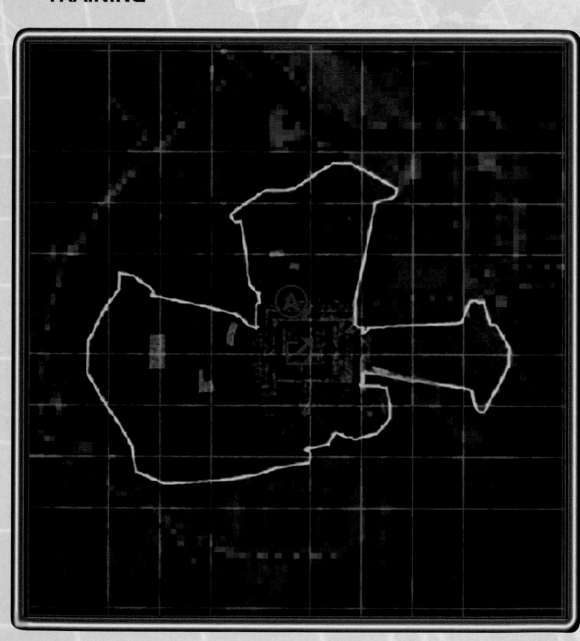

DARREN CHUKITUS

Thanks for taking the time to answer our questions Darren. I'm sure the fans will appreciate your effort.

Tell us a little about yourself. Who are you; how did you get your job; what led you to work on Ghost Recon?

I had been a producer at Red Storm for about 2 years before Ubi Soft bought us. I had produced Rainbow Six: Eagle Watch some years before, so naturally I was excited about working on Ghost Recon because it was creating a new franchise while keeping tactical shooter aspects of the other franchise in place.

To familiarize the audience with your job, please explain what it is that Ubi Soft has you around for. What does a game producer do?

A producer has many roles, all geared around support for the development team. First and foremost is to keep the project running efficiently

continued on page 222

BRIAN REYNOLDS
LEVEL GUY

Life Before Red Storm: Lived in Blacksburg, VA (home of Virginia Tech) and worked a part time job with an architecture/engineering firm. Rode sport bikes on the best twisties this side of the Mississippi. Played a lot of first-person shooters competitively with clans...Very heavy in the Quake scene. Also worked with a mod group (OK, it was just a bunch of friends) called Reactive Software. We made some cool Quake2 mods that never caught on.
Life At Red Storm: Build levels for Ghost Recon. Lobby the powers that be to make our games more like I want them. I usually lose.
Free Time: Playing video games, being insane, wrenching on my car or motorcycle. Not necessarily in that order...insane is usually at the top.
Favorite Comic Book Hero: Rush Limbaugh. There is no way he is actually real.
Favorite Website: www.riceboypage.com
Wisdom For the Masses: Just be yourself, don't worry too much about what other people think. Sounds cliché, but if you want to be happy, it works.
Homepage: www.bossturbo.com

BRIAN UPTON
CHIEF GAME DESIGNER

Life Before Red Storm: Graphics programmer. I started out writing 2-D photo-retouching software, then switched to 3-D.
Life At Red Storm: First I was the VP of Engineering, then I was Director of Game Design, now I've managed to shed all official responsibility and just sit around all day coming up with game ideas.
Free Time: I have two small children—I have almost zero free time. I watch some anime, I play some computer games, I read some history books, occasionally I cut the grass when I think the neighbors are getting annoyed.
Favorite Comic Book Hero: Pupshah.

Favorite Website: www.straightdope.com
Wisdom For the Masses: Don't work for drug addicts.

CHRIS WELLS
CHARACTER ARTIST

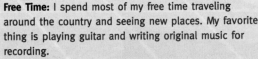

Life Before Red Storm: Lots and lots of drawing!
Life At Red Storm: Really challenging and fun. Always trying to improve my skills...
Free Time: Working out, listening to music, and trying to beat the other Character Artists in Basketball (that'll take a while).
Favorite Comic Book Hero: Batman.
Favorite Website: www.artchive.com
Wisdom For the Masses: Determination is the key to all success. 'Nuff said.

CLARK GIBSON
SOFTWARE ENGINEER

Life Before Red Storm: Attended University of North Carolina studying computer science.
Free Time: I fish the local rivers and play string bass in jazz and bluegrass groups.

CRAIG STALEY
SOFTWARE ENGINEER

Life Before Red Storm: My life was spent in hot, humid Mississippi. I spent a lot of time sweating. I also went to school to learn about those newfangled "computers."
Life At Red Storm: It is less hot and humid. In fact, I am in a dark, cold room. My job is to make the bad guys in the game find you and kill you. Fun, fun.
Free Time: I spend most of my free time stuck in traffic.
Favorite Website: www.theonion.com

DARREN CHUKITUS
PRODUCER

Life Before Red Storm: Doing anything possible to move from rainy Seattle.
Life At Red Storm: Making games and living in Carolina has certainly given my some new perspectives on life. Who could ask for more?

Free Time: I spend most of my free time traveling around the country and seeing new places. My favorite thing is playing guitar and writing original music for recording.
Favorite Comic Book Hero: Marine Boy (Breathe underwater with oxy-gum? Cool!).
Favorite Website: http://www.riffinteractive.com/archive Lessons.htm
Wisdom For the Masses: Do what makes you happy or get happy with what you do.

DAVID HAMM
SOFTWARE ENGINEER

Life Before Red Storm: I grew up in Fort Wayne, Indiana and remain a Midwesterner at heart. I graduated from Harvey Mudd College in '97, which is a small math/science school near LA. Four years was enough of that—both California and school—so I headed East in search of a career in gaming. Thankfully, a kindly senior engineer at RSE considered me a decent gamble.
Life At Red Storm: I spent my first three years at Red Storm working on some of the company's lesser known (non-Rainbow) games. Since then I've been assimilated into the tactical shooter genre. There is always something interesting to work on here. Scripting languages are probably the closest thing I could claim as a specialty.
Free Time: When I'm not coding, I'm usually playing various games with my wife, Mandy, and our insane Jack Russell Terrier, Vader. Other than Red Storm products, I can always count on Blizzard and Id for worthy entertainment. Still playing Starcraft...
Homepage: http://www.cs.hmc.edu/~dhamm/

DEREK L EARWOOD
QA ANALYST

Life Before Red Storm: Varied greatly from dirt farmer to professional sociopath.
Life At Red Storm: Same as above.
Free Time: Everquest, family time, and stuff.
Favorite Comic Book Hero: Danger Mouse.
Favorite Website: Warships1.com
Wisdom For the Masses: Not applicable.

and on schedule. I constantly work with the team and the design department to make sure the original concept of the design is kept in place, and will frequently mediate differing views of features to insure the quality of our game. I will also work as liaison to our third-party contractors, ensuring we are provided with the best services for our product. I guess I'm kind of a jack of all trades.

How did the development of Ghost Recon differ from previous Red Storm titles, like the popular Rogue Spear and Rainbow Six?

Things differ in many ways, but I think that we had more experience put into Ghost Recon than the Rainbow franchise. Red Storm was a new company back then, and I think a lot of us have grown to know tactical shooters and now know better how to make a good game while avoiding the usual burnout associated with making a date for release.

What obstacles arose in the development in Ghost Recon that proved troublesome to solve?

I think it's always hard when you have so many passionate opinions about what the game should play like. The dedication of the team and the respect they've earned through their efforts makes it frequently difficult to decide between whether or not the feature requested is adding to the experience or potentially taking away from it. I tend to take each request very seriously, and try not to dismiss any without a lot of research. Usually our design department scrutinizes the feature and a decision is made that we all will be satisfied with.

continued on page 224

DIANA STELMACK
NETWORK PROGRAMMER

Life Before Red Storm: Like everyone else from Florida, I was born somewhere else. I spent my childhood and college years in Tampa, FL. I was always a nerd, but not a gamer until I met my husband, Greg. I was a Computer Science/Mathematics major at University of South Florida for what seemed to be forever. After graduation, I got married and started working for a Department of Defense contractor, E-Systems. Out of desperation to support his gaming habit, Greg introduced me to a game called Lemmings. After that, I was hooked and he had a better argument for his hardware addiction (his first 3DFX card was so I could play Tomb Raider, and boy it looked cool). He still has to lobby for purchasing new hardware, but he thinks it's easier to get it past me (I don't intend to dispel this illusion).

A year after we married, we relocated to Raleigh, NC. I worked as a contractor at IBM doing Internet Security protocol work, then left for greener pastures at Nortel. I

Engineering Team: (L to R) David Hamm, Jeff Wesevich, Craig Staley, Jon Owen, Clark Gibson, Rob Hunt, Jason Snyder, Joe Sauder, Chris Port, Philip Hebert

DEVELOPMENT TEAM

worked at Nortel doing various network protocol work for telecommunications, starting in ISDN, progressing to Voice Over IP, and ending up in IP Network Management. Recently, for obvious reasons, I decided I had had enough of the Nortel life and knocked on Red Storm's door. The rest is history.

Life At Red Storm: Life at Red Storm includes, as you may have guessed, a lot of gaming. When I'm not programming a game, I am playing a game. It's amazing how fast the day flies by around here. This is probably the fastest pace I've ever worked at and it is awesome. This is also the most fun I've ever had testing my code. Who knew that testing your code in a multiplayer session could be this much fun?

Free Time: Obviously, I spend some of my free time playing games at home, some single-player (Tomb Raider series is my fave) and some multiplayer with my hubby (currently, Diablo II Expansion Pack). When I am not on the computer, I enjoy gardening, cross-stitch, painting ceramics, and, of course, long walks on the beach at sunset.

Favorite Comic Book Hero: Dilbert (Trust me. You know when you've lived the life of Dilbert).

Wisdom For the Masses: Love like you've never been hurt, work like you don't need the money, and dance like nobody's watching...

DION C. ROGERS
LEVEL ARTIST

Life Before Red Storm: Studying Computer Animation and 3D modeling, worked at a company called Random Games for about two years on games such as Microsoft Classic Card Games, Squad Leader, Men Are from Mars Women Are from Venus, and Barbie: Princess Bride! Attending Siggraph conventions, were I learned a lot about computer animation and techniques from people who work in the industry.

Life At Red Storm: Working on low polygon modeling and texture mapping. Enjoying free donuts on Monday mornings, taking advantage of free beverages every three hours, helping myself to free cheese balls and beer on Thursdays! Learning more about game development from my co-workers.

Free Time: Learning more about 3D animation(it's a never ending process), drawing, modeling, and animating, sleeping, hanging out with friends, watching *Austin Powers: The Spy Who Shagged Me* over, and over, and over again. Playing video games, looking forward to buying a Gamecube, playing Munch's Oddysee and learning more Japanese.

Favorite Comic Book Hero: Austin Powers.

Favorite Website: www.oddworld.com

Wisdom For the Masses: Oddworld is a real place, and I know how to get there!

Homepage: http://drop.to/dioncg

ERIC ARMSTRONG
LEAD CHARACTER ARTIST

Life Before Red Storm: I received my BFA in Computer Art and Design from Jacksonville University. Then I worked as an independent contractor for the military in which I generated 3D models and animation for some of their computer-based training software. Afterwards, I got my first job in the games industry out in California. Which finally led me to Red Storm.

Life At Red Storm: Establishing character art pipelines and various techniques that we may incorporate into a given game. I also carry a huge load of the modeling. I created the character models for the original Rainbow Six project. Then I moved on to the ill-fated UFS Vanguard project as a Lead artist, and now Ghost Recon.

Free Time: I really enjoy working out and playing basketball during my free time.

Favorite Comic Book Hero: I don't really get into comic books.

Favorite Website: www.simulatedsports.net

Wisdom For the Masses: Honor God.

ERIC TERRY
ARTIST/
ILLUSTRATOR

Life Before Red Storm: I did the college thing and ended up with a BFA in Illustration from East Carolina University.

Life At Red Storm: Make games look pretty.

If you had to pick one thing that you wish the development team had been able to spend more time/money on, what would it have been?

We had some really good feedback from our focus groups with Ghost Recon, and I think if I had to choose anything, it would be to allow more of these sessions. It was great watching the look on the faces of people who played the game for the first time. The immersion level is high in Ghost Recon, and given time we can always add to that experience.

What do you feel is the most innovative, successfully implemented, or just plain fun feature of Ghost Recon?

We're very proud of many features in Ghost Recon. I would have to say the advances we've made with the AI met most of our expectations. I can say personally that it's a very unsettling experience when you take a shot at a group of enemy soldiers and they try to flank you, drop suppression fire, and launch grenades at you. It gives you the experience of war few games can match.

If you had to pick one single-player campaign mission as your favorite, what would you pick and why?

The swamp mission is very cool. Just for fun I took some specialists equipped with motion sensors and claymores. I'd drop these devices out in the water and move away to wait for the enemy advance. While in my command map I could see them approaching the claymores. This was something out of the movie Aliens. Boom! I was able to take out a large part of the squad. I then used my SAW weapon to lay down suppression fire as the enemy scattered for cover. What an experience.

continued on page 226

Free Time: I spend time with my beautiful, very patient, and loving fiancé Jennifer. Oh, and I play a lot of games and take a lot of macro shots with my digital camera.
Favorite Comic Book Hero: Spiderman.
Favorite Website: www.ebay.com
Wisdom For the Masses: If you don't enjoy what you do, then what's the point?
Homepage: http://home.nc.rr.com/eterry/

GARY STELMACK
ASSISTANT DESIGNER

Life Before Red Storm: A wide variety of jobs while I searched for what I wanted to do when I grew up. Basically pretty boring, until a wonderful opportunity presented itself to me.
Life At Red Storm: A lot of work primarily scripting missions. Also, some time spent coming up with ideas for the next great game, or ways to improve existing ones. Also, a lot of time spent filling my office with monkeys.
Free Time: A variety of activities ranging from Jazzercise to going to Carolina Cobra's games. I also enjoy playing a wide range of electronic games from PC to PS2, and lots of systems in between.
Favorite Comic Book Hero: The Savage Dragon.
Favorite Website: www.redstorm.com. Hey, it is cliché, but I love spending time on our forums, and it is by far the website that I spend the most time on.
Wisdom For the Masses: If you can find and perfect one thing that you do, all others will come easier.

JEFF WESEVICH
SOFTWARE ENGINEER

Life Before Red Storm: 360 Pacific and Atomic Games.
Life At Red Storm: Currently handling audio for Ghost Recon.
Free Time: Variety of things.
Favorite Website: www.bluesnews.com
Wisdom For the Masses: Anyone can get the big stuff generally correct. It takes dedication and hard work to get the details.

DEVELOPMENT TEAM

Engineering Team2: (L to R) David Hamm, Jeff Wesevich, Craig Staley, Jon Owen, Clark Gibson, Rob Hunt, Jason Snyder, Joe Sauder, Chris Port, Philip Hebert

JEREMY BROWN
LEVEL BUILDER

Life Before Red Storm: I attended The Art Institute of Pittsburgh and studied computer animation. While I was there I focused most of my attention on learning 3D Studio Max.

Life At Red Storm: I build 3D environments...and do my best to make them look believable. It's cool.

Free Time: I play guitar, work out, play video games, and hang out with friends.

Favorite Comic Book: Hero Eric Terry.

Favorite Website: http://www.payableondeath.com/

Wisdom For the Masses: Don't be stupid.

JOHN MICHEL
LEVEL BUILDER / RULER OF ALL THAT YOU SEE

Life Before Red Storm: I've lived most of my life in NC, and I grew up mostly in Winston-Salem, pool-hopping and watching movies. I moved to Raleigh to educate myself in the ways of the polygon, and landed a contract job at Virtus Corp making template levels and objects for a couple of game editor programs for some very popular FPSs. After some hard work, persistence, and threats of bodIly harm, I was offered a job at Red Storm to help prepare the world for the way of life that is Force 21.

Life At Red Storm: We're pretty laid back here. Come to think of it, we don't even do a lot of work. Thanks to our tireless engineers, we spent the first two years of Red Storm's existence creating a sweet little computer named "XULU" which has shouldered most of the burden since. Now we spend a month or two entering variables and parameters into XULU, which spends the better part of a year creating our game designs and content. The only reason we keep the artists and engineers on the payroll is for the few little incidents like the Urban Operations fiasco last year. We still don't know how XULU arrived at some of its decisions for that design, but at least we were around to fix it—and we're guaranteed to have plenty of linen textures for future projects if we need them.

Free Time: I still enjoy writing music when I've got time. I have to thank Mr. Nobuo Uematsu for getting me hooked on good game music. I also play a lot of games and collect console systems and games for posterity. One day, I'm sure having three Playstations will be the key to like, saving the world or something. At least that's what I tell my critics.

Favorite Comic Book Hero: Definitely Piccolo. Does that count?

Favorite Website: www.thegia.com. You guys ROCK!

Wisdom For the Masses: I was liberal once. Now I'm educated.

JOHN SONEDECKER
LEAD ARTIST

Life Before Red Storm: Searching for the right career and enjoying life with my wife and Sheltie. Previous careers included food service, retail management, firearms sales and Virtual Reality developer.

Life At Red Storm: I have been proud and lucky enough to be a major part of all the Rainbow Six franchise titles. Now I am helping to forge a new franchise, Ghost Recon. Oh, and a "black op" or two for the company, but I can't talk about them.

If you had to pick one multiplayer map as your favorite, which would you pick and why?

My favorites depend on what type of game we are playing. All maps can be played multiplayer. There is one multiplayer map straight out of Apocalypse Now. It just has that mood generated with the fires burning and the lighting of the area, kind of spooky.

If you had to pick one weapon as your favorite, which would you pick and why?

Again, this is a hard question. I love the sound of an automatic weapon, but I also like the action of an OICW. I find myself using the M4 the most for its accuracy, so it depends on the situation.

What games or game genres, other than any that UbiSoft/Red Storm have worked on, do you like?

Red Storm was my first chance to develop games as producer. I have, however, been friends with people in the industry for 20 years. I remember my friend at Nintendo showing me the prototype of Dragon Warrior. I was hooked right away and have played this franchise since.

Assume for a second that computer games never existed. What do you think you'd be doing now instead of working on Ghost Recon?

I have a great love for music and sound and would probably be much more involved in that area. The chance to take sound and make it interactive has been a great area of joy for me. I believe that the sound in Ghost Recon is some of the most life-like you'll find for this genre.

If you were given unlimited funding and manpower, what kind of game would you want to work on?

continued on page 228

Free Time: Actually I value my free time and do more with my life than just play games. I spend most of my time with my wife and daughter. I love watching my daughter grow and learn. My hobbies include watching and playing ice hockey (the Detroit Red Wings is my family's favorite team), and building plastic military models and dioramas.

Favorite Comic Book Hero: Don't really have a favorite now, but Hagar the Horrible was it growing up.

Wisdom For the Masses: Say what you feel and feel what you say!

JON OWEN
SENIOR ENGINEER

Life Before Red Storm: Most of my youth was spent plinking things with a BB gun in the wilds of Tennessee. After my big can of BB's ran out, I went to the big city to learn about engineering. From engineering, I went to computer science. From computer science, I wound up working for Virtus, doing the hydrodynamics code for the submarines in Tom Clancy's SSN. It was a short hop to Red Storm.

Life At Red Storm: I've been dying to work on a first person shooter ever since Wolfenstein 3D. Now I am. Life is good.

Free Time: Everquest, browsing Everquest websites, and talking about Everquest.

Favorite Comic Book Hero: The Tick, 'cause he says things like: "I don't know the meaning of the word surrender! I mean, I know it, I'm not dumb...just not in this context."

Favorite Website: http://www.seanbaby.com

Wisdom For the Masses: A good plan, violently executed now, is better than a perfect plan next week. George S. Patton, General (1885-1945)

KAREEM LEGGETT
LEVEL ARTIST

Life Before Red Storm: Sitting around in a dirty T-shirt staring at a monitor in a dimly lit room while playing games.

Life At Red Storm: Sitting around in a clean T-shirt staring at a monitor in a dimly

DEVELOPMENT TEAM

lit room while playing games.

Free Time: I patrol the city fighting crime as my alter ego, "Fancy Lad."

Favorite Comic Book Hero: Uhhh, Superman I guess.

Favorite Website: www.vir2l.com

Wisdom For the Masses: If you are looking for sewer textures, and the link says "Manhole," for god's sake don't click on it!

Homepage: www.denzel-washington.com

KIM KIRCHSTEIN
TEXTURE ARTIST

Life Before Red Storm: I attended East Carolina University's School of Art, where I earned (REALLY earned) a BFA in Surface Design. I then designed upholstery fabric for the world's top upholstery design companies for a few years...um, that wasn't the world o' fun it might sound like...so I did some freelance art for a while...

Life At Red Storm: Now THIS is fun! Having a great time

Engineering Team3: (Top Row L to R) Rob Hunt, Craig Staley, Chris Port, Jason Snyder, Joe Sauder, Jon Owen, Jeff Wesevich. (Bottom Row L to R): Clark Gibson, Philip Hebert, David Hamm

doing work I REALLY enjoy!!

Free Time: Listening to lots of loud, often raucous music...going to see bands...taking photographs...using too much punctuation...

Favorite Comic Book Hero: Jimmy Corrigan (yes, he IS a comic superhero) and, of course, Batman.

Favorite Website: A couple guys here introduced me to www.ebay.com and now I'm hooked...(grr...). I also like www.onionheadmonster.com (for fun!)

Wisdom For the Masses: Two things: First, LAUGH at everything you can, or else... and, second, The ad that says "Ancient Chinese secret, huh...??..." is an ad for Calgon fabric softener.

MATTHIAS DOHMEN
ASSISTANT GAME DESIGNER

Life Before Red Storm: Playing games. Playing lots of games. Playing lots and lots of games. Etc. It's really a fine blend of playing tabletop RPGS, CCGS, PC games, console games, board games, watching movies, reading a ton, building PC systems, working as tech support, and a sprinkling of network administration—mixed with writing tabletop RPG adventures and game overviews in my spare time (which turned out not to be in vain). I think there was some sort of formal education in there somewhere, but one never can tell.

Life At Red Storm: Making the very best tactical FPS ever takes up most of my time here. I also am constantly learning design philosophies and methods and figuring out how to apply them to game concepts—a process which I never plan to cease.

Free Time: My free time is taken up by my fiancé Leonor, who plays games, and aside from her there's...well...games. I also occasionally play games, but that's only when I'm not playing games.

Favorite Comic Book Hero: Batman. No superpowers, just trauma-based insanity and tights. You have to respect that.

Favorite Website: www.somethingawful.com

Wisdom For the Masses: Never give up! Well, actually, give up the useless things, but never give up the important things. It helps if you can tell the difference between useless and important things.

It would be a game with unlimited ability. A lot of us in the industry imagine a virtual space similar to the holodeck on Star Trek. Any type of game that has unlimited ability to tap into all your senses and be completely immersing.

If you had a bunch of free space in a book to say anything (like now), what would you say?

I hope that Ghost Recon provides as much fun to the player as it was for us to make. We have an incredible staff at Red Storm, and we take great pride in developing games for gamers. We believe we've hit the mark with this title.

For all the players out there, if there is one tactic/strategy/hint you could give them that you feel is the most important, or just really useful/cool, what would you tell them?

Develop your team management skills while playing this game. There are unlimited ways to reach your objectives. Work to explore different ways through your teams to find the best tactical strategies. This will offer you hours of fun.

MICHAEL "KAMIKAZE" COSNER
ANIMATION/ CINEMATICS DESIGNER

Life Before Red Storm:
Attempted to pursue "real" career goals that would satisfy my parent's wishes. Failed miserably. Decided to pursue my own career goals. Succeeded admirably. Joined up with some unlikely cohorts to form Red Storm Entertainment, and the rest, as they say, is history.
Life At Red Storm: An incredibly exciting and invigorating experience, at least, until the power goes out and you realize that your UPS doesn't work. Then it blows.
Free Time: Playing drums, doing improv, studying Torite Jutsu (martial arts), and harboring an unhealthy obsession with my 5-year-old Orbitz drink.
Favorite Comic Book Hero: Sam Keith's The MAXX.
Favorite Website: www.theonion.com
Wisdom For the Masses: "A severed foot is the ultimate stocking stuffer." – Mitch Hedberg
Homepage: www.idiotlogic.com

MIKE D HAYNES
LEAD ARTIST

Life Before Red Storm: I've worked at a lot of places before Red Storm. Here's the list: Healthy Harvest maintenance guy, Highland Farms dishwasher, Ingle's grocery bag boy, Blk Mtn office supply delivery boy, Comfort Inn supply guy, Western Steer cook, Western Steer meat cutter, Beacon Blanket company, Denny's Restaurant, Town of Montreat maintenance crew, Ryan's Steakhouse meat cutter, Raging Waters life guard, Security guard, Kroger floor cleaner, UPS shipping, Random Games, Interactive Simulations, and now Red Storm.
Life At Red Storm: It's great, I've been here for three years now. Everyone is extremely talented and seems to enjoy what they are doing. I can't decide if it's because they enjoy their work, or if it's the free soda.

Level Artists: (L to R): Tim Alexander, John Sonedecker, Eric Terry, Dion Rogers, Jeremy Brown, Suzanne Meiler, Kim Kirchstein, John Michel, Brian Reynolds, Kareem Leggett

Free Time: Hanging out with my wife Mir, traveling, playing guitar, playing video games, animation, hang gliding, ice climbing, bungie jumping, sky diving, ice sculpting, mind games, penguin rescue, making up stories...
Favorite Website: www.phenomstudios.com
Wisdom For the Masses: "When you go ice-skating, try not to swing your arms too much, because that really annoys me." - Jack Handey

PHILIP HEBERT
SOFTWARE ENGINEER

Life Before Red Storm: Graduated from Georgia Tech with a bachelor degree in Computer Science.
Life At Red Storm: Worked on Rainbow Six and Rogue Spear. Current project is Ghost Recon.
Free Time: I play FPS games and shoot handguns.
Favorite Website: www.voodooextreme.com

ROBERT HUNT
SOFTWARE ENGINEER

Life Before Red Storm: Lots of school, lots of programming.

Life At Red Storm: Lots of programming still. Mostly doing user interface work or some odd derivative. Everything is fun and games till you have to make something persistent.
Free Time: Playing computer games, reading, getting outdoors. The three basic things.
Favorite Comic Book Hero: Spiderman.
Favorite Website: www.fas.org
Wisdom For the Masses: 5% fruit juice is better than none.

SLOAN ELLIOT ANDERSON
ARTIST

Life Before Red Storm: First, a starving musician (well...not really). Shortly thereafter, I realized that a computer and moderate artistic skill could land me a real job! After a one-year bout in Web Design, I was hired on here at Red Storm.
Life At Red Storm: 2D Art. UI (User Interface) and Textures occupy most of my "work" schedule, though I'll admit that the majority of my time is spent arguing with Engineering and Design.
Free Time: Music, mostly (writing, performing, recording, etc.). Sound Engineering is an exceptionally large hobby (and secondary source of income) of mine; I record a lot of local musicians in my home studio.
Favorite Comic Book Hero: Captain America...?
Favorite Website: http://www.estudio.com
Wisdom For the Masses: "If it weren't for electricity, we'd all be watching television by candlelight."
--George Gobel

SUZANNE MEILER
LEVEL ARTIST

Life Before Red Storm: I attended the School of Communication Arts and went on to work at Random Games. I was there for about a year and was an artist on a turn-based game called Squad Leader. Let me tell you making a turn-based game is not fun, I needed 3D!
Life At Red Storm: Fantastic! I work with a great group

UI, FX, Multiplayer Artists: (L to R): Ray Tylak, Mike Haynes, Yongha Hwang, Demond Rogers, Sloan Anderson

of talented people and have learned so much about game development from each of them. We are doing some awesome games and its so exciting to see it all come together. The best part is seeing your game in the store; I can't even begin to express how that feels!

Free Time: Mostly at the beach, if I could I would live in Wilmington, N.C.! I like to shop, but what girl doesn't? I enjoy hanging out with my friends and watching any of Mark Wahlberg's movies!

Favorite Comic Book Hero: Barbie?

Favorite Website: www.mtv.com (I love *The Real World*)

Wisdom For the Masses: "You can't always get what you want, but if you try sometimes you just might find you get what you need." The Rolling Stones.

THOMAS DEVRIES
ARTIST / DESIGNER / CINEMATIC CREATOR

Life Before Red Storm: When I was five or six I decided I either wanted to be an astronaut or a comic book artist when I grew up. I ditched the idea of being an astronaut because I was afraid of cutting my golden locks and decided on becoming a, *gasp*, professional artist. Call me tenacious, but I stuck to my guns, and actually decided that my goal in going to college was to hone my painting skills so that I could become a coveted comic cover artist. In the fall '91, I started at East Carolina University. I chose that school because they had a reputation as being both a great Fine Arts school and great Music school (I'm a classically trained bassist—like how I dropped that in!). Anyway, my first day there I met my one and only roommate that I had in School: Eric Terry (GR level texture artist). In the first college class I ever had I immediately became fast friends with Jonathan Peedin (Red Storm's very own Art Director). I thought he was cool, because he also liked Jim Lee's work on the X-men (which actually does make you a very cool person). It's funny, but over time, most of my artist friends from college and one from High school are now working with me here, which is a blast. During my college years, I managed to play in a couple of bands, get published in a local comic book anthology, win a fellowship for a Yale summer painting program, and start working on the first ever video-taped WW2 war epic with my friend Jeff McFadyen (also works here). One day I'll finish the editing/post-production on this already American classic movie entitled "Into the Eagles Nest." Strangely enough, I would have completed work on it, but I started work at Red Storm and have been too busy ever since—but I swear one day it will be done!

P.S. did you notice how I mentioned I went to Yale? I like to believe this gives me the right to be—nay, *demands* that I be—a snob (which I am). Now I only use Grey Poupon on my sam-iches.

Life At Red Storm: Currently I'm working on Ghost Recon as a character designer and Texture Artist. Although I was one of the original people on this project, I left to work on another game for over a year and only recently came back onto what had become Ghost Recon. Ever since I've been back on the game, I've been working really hard with the other character artists and our Russian military advisor to redesign the characters, making them some of the most accurately detailed and distinctive characters ever in a 3D military game. Beyond that, at the moment I tend to stick my nose into a lot of other aspects of the game. What can I say? There's just so much about this game that excites me that I don't want to miss out on any of the fun of producing all of its component pieces.

Free Time: I try to see every movie that comes out, compose music, play my bass/guitar/keyboards/drums, play games, play with kittens, read, customize 12-inch action figures, and go out on the weekends to do some dancing and drinking in the vain hope that I will find a wife so that I won't die broken and alone.

Favorite Comic Book Hero: It's a toss up between Wolverine and Kitty FuFu.

Favorite Website: I'm not sure I should to tell you my favorite.

Wisdom For the Masses: "David, I will break." – Teddy

Homepage: http://www.geocities.com/thomas _d121/index.html

my time at wrong career in crazy New York City.

Life At Red Storm: Enjoying the peaceful life with family and animals here in Morrisvillle, NC. Just had our first baby... It's a BOY!

Free Time: I will generate more family members to get a bigger tax return.

Favorite Comic Book Hero: Too many to list.

Favorite Website: Too many to list.

Wisdom For the Masses: What you do in life echoes throughout eternity... and as my wife always says, don't forget to leave the toilet seat down.

Homepage: http://y42.photos.yahoo.com/bc/yongha88/slideshow?&.dir=/Yahoo!+Photo+Album/Eugene%27s+album&.src=ph&.view=t

TIM ALEXANDER
MAN OF MANY HATS

Life Before Red Storm: I spent much of my time in transit.

Life At Red Storm: Working at Redstorm is a satisfying blend of new challenges and interesting people. North Carolina is a beautiful state.

Free Time: After work, travel has always been high on my list of priorities. Europe, Asia, Africa, and of course the Glorious United States of America.

Favorite Comic Book Hero: That one guy with the exaggerated musculature. You know the one. Somethin' Man...

Favorite Website: www.cgchannel.com

Wisdom For the Masses: To be an American citizen is a privilege unlike any other. Go out and see for yourself if you can. The best part of travel is coming home.

YONGHA HWANG
3D ARTIST

Life Before Red Storm: Born in Seoul, South Korea, Served unnecessary military service over two years. Arrived in US 1995. Enjoyed school life in upstate New York and wasted